Introductory Guide to Midwest Antiques

By Marlene Semple

Greatlakes Living Press, Publishers, Matteson, Illinois

Introductory Guide to Midwest Antiques
©Marlene Semple 1976
All rights reserved
Printed in U.S.A.
International Standard Book Number: 0-915498-17-0
Library of Congress Catalog Card Number: 75-41638

Cover design by Joseph Mistak, Jr.
Cover photo by Ron Nielsen
Illustrations by Chris Avers and Dale Beda

Greatlakes Living Press
3634 W. 216th Street
Matteson, Illinois 60443

Contents

You've probably guessed that if you already know a great deal about antiques, this book isn't for you. And I'm not going to pose as an expert. I didn't know anything about antiques until I came to the Midwest a few years ago. At that time I was faced with the problem of furnishing both an office and a city apartment. The only real assets I had were a craving for surroundings I could feel comfortable with, a growing interest in things of the past, and so few bucks in the bank that I was forced into being resourceful.

A friend of mine—I don't know how *he* became interested in antiques—told me about a marvelous lady who, together with her husband, maintain an antique shop in the basement of their home. My friend and I went to the shop one weekend afternoon. All I spent was $6 for a coat rack, but I was hooked.

A few days later, I went to the library to get a book on Midwest antiques and found there was nothing specific on the subject. There are several books on antiques, even some on Victorian furniture, but nothing that seemed to coordinate with my experience. I checked a number of bookstores and found the same situation. And that is how this book came to be. I started doing research to satisfy my personal need and then began to think that there might be others whom my research might benefit.

I realize that this book only scratches the surface. The study of antiques is as vast and complex as history, of which, of course, it is a department. But we have to start somewhere, right?

I remember a brief conversation I had with George Harrison Daniels of the Harrison-Davis Trading Co., Inc., an antique warehouse in Chicago. I told him I was gathering material for a book on Midwest antiques.

"What kind of book are you going to write?" he asked. "Scholarly? Popular?"

"Popular," I replied.

"Good," he said. "Don't spoil a fun subject."

I tried not to.

Marlene Semple

Chicago
January, 1976

Foreword

- If you like hand-thrown pottery, handmade quilts, old buildings, and macrame, you'll probably like old furniture.

- If your life is constantly changing, if you somehow yearn for permanence in the midst of all the impermanence around us, you can find it in old furniture.

- If you're tired of built-in obsolescence in the things you buy for your home and office, you're ready for the constancy of antiques.

- If you're looking for a good investment, you might consider antiques, now rated the seventh best investment—up from tenth a few years ago.

- If you want furnishings that are easy to live with, reasonable in price, well-made, and a cinch to take care of, you should buy antiques.

But if you live or shop in the Midwest and you're a novice at antiques, you probably don't know where or how to start collecting. Not that there aren't a lot of antiques and near-antiques in the Midwest. There are. Shops are stuffed with objects culled from Victorian town and farm houses. But little information about these furnishings is available to the novice collector. This is so, in part, because Victorian furniture only recently reached the venerable stage, and even books that deal seriously with Victoriana discuss almost exclusively products that were made in the East or in Europe. There are very few references to styles and pieces that were made and can still be found in the Midwest, which bloomed during the Victorian era and which still retains in many localities something of the aesthetic flavor of the Victorian times.

From time to time, an article on Midwest antiques appears in a local newspaper, but restrictions of space and time usually dictate a superficial treatment of only a part of the subject, and it would take years to collect enough of these articles to constitute a reliable reference. Antique dealers and shopkeepers are usually cooperative about answering questions, but sometimes their knowledge is sketchy, or the customer does not ask the right questions.

At the very least, this book will help you ask the right questions. It might even push you toward a lifelong avocation or even a career.

Acknowledgments

My sincere appreciation to the many individual dealers and collectors who have shared their knowledge with me as I gathered the material for this book.

Special thanks to the cooperative people at the official agencies I contacted, in particular, staff members at the Chicago Historical Society, the Missouri Historical Society, the State of Wisconsin Vacation and Travel Service, the Minnesota Department of Economic Development, the Grand Rapids Public Museum, Grand Rapids, Michigan, and the Canadian Consulate and Office of Tourism in Chicago.

And profound gratitude to my husband for his continuing help, support, and encouragement.

I would also like to thank Ruth and John Tuzson for the use of their 1885 home in Illinois, as background for the back cover photograph.

How a Young Couple in an Old Apartment Furnished Six Rooms for $1300

Lucy and Jim, a couple in their early thirties, are moving from a rented studio apartment to a 60-year old condominium building. The apartment for which they have signed mortgage papers has seven rooms—living room, dining room, three bedrooms, kitchen, and sunporch (and two bathrooms, which for some reason aren't counted).

At present, their furniture consists of a sofa bed covered in velvet with stripes of white and browns, an arm chair of brown Naugahyde, a white enamel ice cream table and two chairs, a big old chest of drawers that came from the attic of Lucy's aunt and some large floor pillows. There is also an easel, which Lucy uses when she brings work home from the publishing house where she works as a book designer. Jim teaches English literature at a large university in Chicago. They are confirmed city dwellers.

It is obvious to Jim and Lucy that when they move from a one-room apartment to a seven-room apartment they are going to need six more rooms of furniture. So they begin spending Saturdays and evenings visiting furniture stores. They soon realize the frustrating position they are in. Lucy and Jim value quality and are concerned about esthetics, but they have only $1500 in the bank for furniture. It's not enough, and they are shocked at how much more good furniture costs now than it did even just a few years ago, when they bought some things for their studio apartment. They could easily spend their $1500 decorating their living room with fashionable, well-made furniture. But what would they do with the other six rooms?

Neither Lucy nor Jim foresee their incomes jumping dramatically in the future. What they buy will have to last for a long time.

So they decide to set their sights a little lower than the illustrations

1

in *House Beautiful*, and they start shopping around for "popular-priced" furniture. In this category, vinyl veneers and molded polystyrene often replace the solid wood and sturdy veneers of good quality furniture. But Jim and Lucy become aware that many manufacturers of this furniture don't subscribe to the late Mies van der Rohe's famous maxim: "Less is more." More is better, these manufacturers believe, and they try to prove it by covering up poor construction with fussy designs and tacky upholstery fabrics.

Confused, Jim and Lucy back off; they buy nothing. They move their roomful of furniture into their condominium, where their footsteps echo in high-ceilinged rooms, and their visitor's principal comment is: "My, what a big apartment!"

Meanwhile, Lucy and Jim are trying out the restaurants in their "new" neighborhood. They discover that there are few new buildings, except along the lakefront where skyrocketing land values too often bring about the destruction of unprofitable (at least by today's standards) older, smaller buildings, which are replaced by towering highrise apartments. Away from the lake the couple find many turn-of-the-century buildings, and restaurateurs have capitalized on the special atmosphere of some of the old places, planning the decor around what is already there, rather than gutting the buildings and turning them into modern plastic palaces.

Lucy and Jim succumb to the charm of the bentwood furniture, the Tiffany-style lamps, and the Boston ferns of these new-old restaurants. Thus primed, they return one Sunday from brunch at such restaurant and wander into an antique store that displays a chest of drawers similar to the one they own, which came from the attic of Lucy's aunt. It's oak, they are told, made around 1880, and is priced at $185. And here, the shopkeeper points, is a bedstead from the same period. Doesn't need refinishing, just a wiping down with linseed oil. A good buy at $60.

Sixty dollars? Jim and Lucy look at each other. They can afford $60—even the $180 it will take to buy springs and mattress to go with the bedstead. And they *are* getting tired of sleeping on the sofa bed. The deal is made. They will borrow Jim's brother's station wagon and pick up the bedstead next week.

Now, Lucy comments, if we just had something to store sweaters and blankets in, we could stop worrying about furnishing our bedroom.

Look at that old trunk, Jim says—it still has an immigrant's Swedish-American line stickers on it. And the leather handles are in good shape. We could use that for a storage chest, and it's only $25. Lucy agrees; it's a good idea.

Their next purchase is an oak rocker, *circa* 1900, with a design pressed into the wood at the back. Although in good condition structurally, the rocker needs to be refinished. In this case, they learn, refinishing means stripping off the old stain and varnish and replacing same, but the shopowner assures them this will not be a hard job. If he refinishes it for them, the rocker will cost $85. They buy it "as is" for $40.

By this time, Jim and Lucy have given up the idea of furnishing their home within three months, as they had hoped. For one thing, since they are shopping on a piece-by-piece basis, "antiquing" is taking large chunks out of their weekends. But it also is taking on the characteristics of a hobby, and they don't want to make work out of it by pushing themselves. Also, they don't want to decide hastily on pieces that might turn out to be mistakes. They aren't worried about being "taken," because they have learned that, in the price category they're dealing in, it's not worth the trouble for someone to manufacture fakes. True, prices may vary from dealer to dealer—say from $5 to $50 for a certain type of item—but the prices marked on articles in shops are mostly fair, they feel.

They do want to be sure that they actually *like* an item before they buy it, because they feel they are investing more than money—something of themselves—especially if they will have to refinish the piece. Besides, they plan to live with each of their selections for a long time.

They have heard of people who collect a houseful of old furniture, resell it all and start over, making money and indulging their acquisitive instinct at the same time. These people are not dealers, really, but they're certainly more sophisticated antiquarians than Jim and Lucy. At this stage, they wouldn't think of selling their carefully chosen pieces.

As the weeks pass, their dining room begins to bother them. Their ice cream table is in the kitchen, and the dining room is large and empty. To carry out the turn-of-the-century Golden Oak period, which they find attractive, they decide to look for a round oak table with a pedestal base and six chairs. Tables in this style have become something of a fad in the past few years, and prices are beginning to climb. In one of their favorite in-town antique shops, a refinished specimen is priced at $350, and the chairs are extra. Lucy and Jim decide this is too much, and take off for a weekend in the country.

On the way to Galena, Illinois, an old riverboat town that has at least 30 antique shops, they find a table *and* six chairs for $300, and the set won't need refinishing for another 20 years—well, maybe 10 years. The dealer makes regular trips to Chicago and will deliver their purchases to their apartment. A few months later, they buy a medium-sized oak sideboard for $225, and they aren't bothered anymore by the dining room.

Lucy and Jim once thought they would like a brass bed in their second bedroom. They had heard brass beds were becoming coveted items and felt that guests who slept in one would feel pampered. But they have found that double-sized brass beds are now bringing $350 to $450, and they are reconsidering. In Galena, they find a substitute—a rather delicate-looking iron bedstead, made during the same period as the brass beds. The price tag was $30. To refinish this bedstead, they smooth off the old paint using a wire-brush attachment on an electric drill, and then spray-paint it with white enamel. They add to the room a small wicker table ($25), a dark-stained bentwood chair ($15), and an early Victorian mirror ($40). They decide their guests can do without a dresser (how often do you use one in a motel?) and, as a substitute, they simply cover the generous shelves of the closet with adhesive shelf paper.

After pricing a roll-top desk at $325, Jim and Lucy visit a second-hand office furniture store. They poke around for an hour or so in a third-floor storeroom, then choose a mahogany desk with decorative brass drawer pulls for $30. It is probably only about 50 years old, but with a Marshall Field & Company nameplate on the inside of the middle drawer, it is, they decide, a worthwhile investment. A desk chair costs them $8. Considerable browsing in antique shops turns up a Globe Company three-drawer oak filing cabinet for $50. Now if they can just find an old green eyeshade . . .

Jim and Lucy figure they have so far spent only $1050, including the paint and other refinishing materials (but not including the electric drill and attachments) and are entitled to a little frivolity. So, on a vacation trip to Door County, Wisconsin, when they come across a day bed from the late American Empire period (mid-1800s), they cheerfully pay the $85, and load it in the station wagon they have rented. They know they should avoid buying upholstered pieces, because rehabilitating them is so expensive, but they calculate that the $150 more that they will spend to fix up the daybed will be well worth it. In fact, if they are careful to buy sturdy, soil-resistant upholstery fabric, the daybed will give them 10 or 15 years of service before it has to be recovered again. An unusual but useful piece, it will always be worth at least as much as the purchase price.

Next comes a stroke of real luck. The long-established publishing company where Lucy works has a surplus furniture sale. For $25 apiece, she picks up two stacking oak bookcases of 1910 vintage. She is careful to treat the matter off-handedly. After all, why should she tell the world that a couple of weeks before she had seen similar book-cases priced at $150 each?

Thus, for an investment of $1300, Jim and Lucy now have acquired old furniture worth about $1000 more, and they can expect it to in-crease in value at a rate of 10 to 15 percent a year. With the $200 they have left in their furniture fund, they can buy a new rug for the living room. They will probably choose carpeting in a floral pattern or a machine-made copy of a Persian rug, imported from Europe—an in-expensive wool floor covering that is widely available in department stores.

Of course, their apartment is not absolutely *stuffed* with furniture as it would have been in Victorian times, but clutter and ostentatious-ness were some of the worst characteristics of the period, not the ones we want to emulate. Actually, it is easier to appreciate a few carefully chosen pieces than a hodgepodge of woods, fabrics, and designs. In this case, less certainly *is* more.

And besides, Lucy and Jim want to leave some space for Boston ferns.

How the Midwest Furniture Industry Grew

As long ago as the 1930s, when Easterners were caught up in a fad for colonial furniture, Midwesterners were collecting the Victorian furniture of the early settlers, and many people were able to retrieve old pieces from attics and basements of their family homes. Today, Easterners are still intrigued by colonial styles, although the popularity of Victorian furniture is growing, even along the Atlantic seaboard.

In the Midwest, colonial furniture just doesn't seem appropriate. The architecture of the old Midwestern buildings is Victorian—there are virtually none older than that. And some lucky Midwesterners are still unearthing Victorian relics from family homesteads. The rest of us are scouring the countryside as well as the city streets for anything made at least 50 years ago. Those in the know realize that furniture that's now between 50 and 100 years old is in the category that will increase most in value within the next few years. In particular, furniture in the styles of Eastlake, Mission, Golden Oak, and Art Nouveau—all of which you'll be able to recognize after you read the next few chapters—are the best bets for making money on antique investments.

The 19th century was a time of great expansion, of innovation, and, particularly in the Midwest, a period of blossoming. At the beginning of the century, the westward movement of the pioneers was as yet only a trickle through the Cumberland Gap into Kentucky and down the Ohio River from Pittsburgh. There were relatively few settlers west of the Appalachians.

Most of those who had moved on into the Midwest were trappers, hunters, miners, and farmers. There were also artisans, shopkeepers, traders, doctors. Not a few were jacks of all trades, masters of several. Abraham Lincoln, born in 1809, became, in turn, a farmhand, boatman, storekeeper, postmaster, surveyor, militia captain, lawyer, state

Country furnituremakers adapted styles to their own needs and abilities.

Traditional Chippendale chair
made by master craftsman, 18th c.

Chippendale-style chair
made by country
craftsman, 18th c.

Pine desk showing Norwegian influence, made in Minnesota about 1835.

legislator, congressman, President. Although his career reached unusual heights, its diversity was not unusual for a frontiersman.

Most of the very early settlers were Anglo-Americans. Not for a few decades would great numbers of Germans, Scandinavians, and other Europeans emigrate to the Midwest. In the wilderness, the pioneers built homes and other buildings—at first, of logs, later, of clapboard. The first furniture was as crude as the first shelters. Beds, tables, and chairs were of prime importance. Until cupboards and bureaus could be built or bought, the settlers' traveling trunks served as storage pieces. These, and a few small items such as dishes and silverware, and perhaps a clock, were all the household furnishings most pioneers could take with them.

Many settlers made simple furniture for their own use. Although much country-made furniture was of plain design and made of local woods, the pieces that survive have a charm that is all the more appealing to us today. In fact, these "primitive" pieces made by people who were not professional cabinetmakers are greatly sought after by collectors today.

For more sophisticated pieces, there always seemed to be professional woodworkers around—cabinetmakers or joiners who made furniture to order or sold from stock they kept on hand. The virgin forests of the Midwest, soon to be cleared for farms and commerce, beckoned to those who worked with wood, although newly arrived cabinetmakers sometimes advertised that they had brought with them a supply of mahogany for fine furniture. In 1818, *The Emigrant's Guide to the Western and Southwestern States and Territories* reassuringly stated that "Tables, chairs, and bedsteads are made in all the large towns in the valleys of Ohio and Mississippi, with all the requisite qualities of elegance and strength."

In Indiana, for instance, there seems to have been enough cabinetmakers to supply the needs of the settlers from 1820 on. In 1840, furnituremaking ranked third among Indiana industries, after the construction and leather industries.

Some cabinetmakers and joiners were itinerants. They took up residence at a local boardinghouse or with a family that had a spare bed, and they worked in a town until the needs of the people were met. Then they moved on to another town. Cabinetmakers who settled down often made their business a family affair, the sons, in particular, taking up the careers of their fathers.

In these early years cabinetmakers not only made furniture, but various tools and machine parts. Betty Lawson Walters, in her study entitled *Furniture Makers of Indiana, 1793 to 1850*, lists the following items of furniture that were made by woodworkers of the period: beds, bookcases, bureaus, chairs, chests, clock cases, coffins, commodes, cradles, cribs, cupboards, desks, dressers, lockers, looking glasses, pianos, presses (china and clothes), secretaries, settees, sideboards, "sociables," sofas, stands, stools, tables, wardrobes, and miscellaneous. "Miscellaneous" included literally everything from wash sinks to bird cages, checkers, parts for printing presses, and sausage stuffers.

Making coffins was an important part of many woodworking businesses. Some cabinetmakers took up undertaking as a sideline, and a few eventually became morticians in preference to the less steady trade of cabinetmaking.

As in the cities of the East, there was in the Midwest a range of style, elegance, and price in furniture produced by cabinetmakers. The newly emigrated cabinetmakers made furniture in the styles they had known in the East, and with just as much talent as they had in the East, adapting their products to the needs and pocketbooks of their pioneer neighbors. Although there were some regional differences in furniture made locally in the early 19th century, these differences became less marked as years passed. By midcentury, they were almost nonexistent, except in the primitive pieces.

Until the beginning of the period covered in this book, practically all the furniture used in the Midwest was made in the Midwest. Only the wealthy could and did import furniture by boat from Europe and the cities of the eastern seaboard. But as steamboat traffic increased, furniture was shipped in quantity to the Midwest, first from Cincinnati and Pittsburgh, then, later, from New York, Boston, Philadelphia, and New Orleans. St. Louis, which had commercial ties to the East since its earliest settlement, was an important distribution point for goods coming to the West and Midwest.

From the late 1820s, the Allegheny Chair Manufacturing Company in Pittsburgh supplied chairs and settees for thousands of Ohio River steamboats and hotels. In 1829, the Cincinnati Chair Manufactory advertised "fancy Grecian drawing room and Windsor chairs and lounges equal in every respect to those made in the Atlantic cities . . . the greatest variety of chairs in the Western Country." Cincinnati was also the chief source of furniture for planters in the South.

While the great westward movement continued, changes occurred as a result of the Industrial Revolution, in the new settlements as well

Boston rocker with fiddleback
design, Indiana, 1850.

Early versions of the rocking chair, as
interpreted by Midwestern country craftsmen.

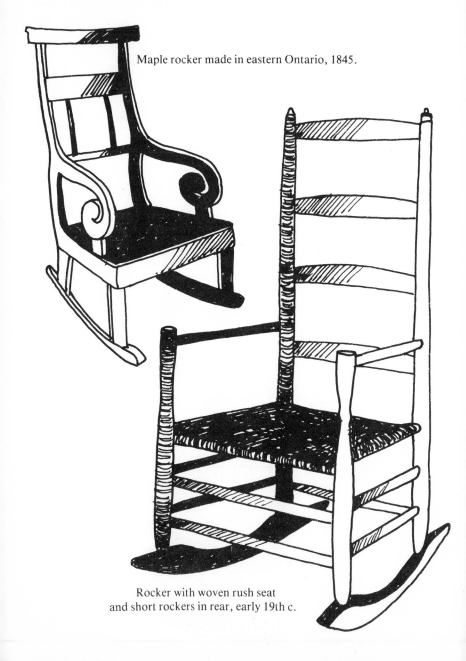

Maple rocker made in eastern Ontario, 1845.

Rocker with woven rush seat
and short rockers in rear, early 19th c.

as in the old. The earliest cabinetmakers in the Midwest considered themselves fortunate if they possessed a turning lathe. In the 1830s and 1840s machinery powered by dogs, horses, or water became more common. Furnituremakers began to cluster their shops (some of which by then were approaching the status of factories) along rivers to make use of water power for their machinery.

This was the reason for the founding of the furniture industry in Grand Rapids, Michigan, a small town that would eventually become the furniture capital of the world. Grand Rapids, a town 100 miles north of the Indiana border and 30 miles east of Lake Michigan, at first huddled along the Grand River, which drops eight feet through the rapids there. Originally, several Indian trails converged in the area, because the river could be forded at that point.

In 1836 a cabinetmaker named William ("Deacon") Haldane arrived in Grand Rapids from New York by way of Ohio. Haldane is credited with being the first Grand Rapids furnituremaker, and a Windsor chair that he built is the only early Grand Rapids piece that has been positively identified. It is now in the Grand Rapids Public Museum.

The following year regular steamship schedules were set up, and

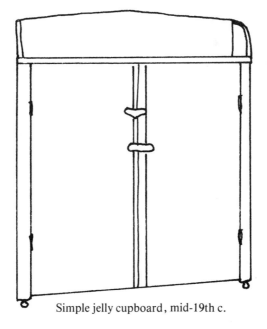

Simple jelly cupboard, mid-19th c.

goods from Grand Rapids were shipped downriver to Grand Haven, and from there to other points, notably Chicago and Milwaukee. By 1840, a dozen cabinet, chair, and related woodworking businesses were clustered in a small area in town near the river. Attracted by the abundant supply of lumber from the Michigan forests, the availability of water for power and transportation, and the needs of a growing population, more woodworkers set up shop in Grand Rapids. Soon, the local need for furniture was being met, and Grand Rapids business-men began looking elsewhere for markets. As early as 1851, William Powers and E.M. Ball shipped 10,000 chairs to Chicago during a calendar year.

For 20 years, water was the only satisfactory conveyor of transpor-tation through Grand Rapids, and shipping was not possible during the winter months when the river was frozen over. Nor was there a good road or railroad. In 1855 a plank road was completed as far as Kalamazoo. The Panic of 1857 delayed the completion of the Detroit and Milwaukee Railroad line to Grand Rapids, but it was finally finished in July, 1858, and greeted exuberantly by the inhabitants. Seven weeks later the line reached its ultimate point, Grand Haven, on the eastern shore of Lake Michigan. The *Grand Rapids Daily Eagle* then announced, somewhat optimistically, "We are now but a few hours' distance from everywhere."

In Deacon Haldane's early days, most furniture was made entirely by hand. Then, in 1840, the steam-driven band saw was invented. It was able to cut out intricate curves from any thickness of wood. Dur-ing the next decade, this and other steam-driven machines freed furni-turemakers from the necessity of having their shops adjacent to a source of water power. Hence the number of furniture factories in the Midwest increased dramatically, with Cincinnati and Grand Rapids becoming the leading furniture centers for the Midwest, South, and West.

The scroll-footed furniture of the 1840s was admirably suited to factory production. Indeed, some people have accused John Hall, the Baltimore architect who created the scroll style, of designing furniture specifically for that reason. In these years also, what was called in the Midwest the "French antique" and "French rococo' styles were be-coming popular. As machinery improved, the carving of these styles became more intricate, reaching the ultimate in the overelaborate pieces made in John Belter's shops in New York.

Because of the new mass production techniques, factory-made fur-niture became widely available at prices the independent cabinetmaker

Cherry cupboard made by Shakers in Ohio, late 19th c.

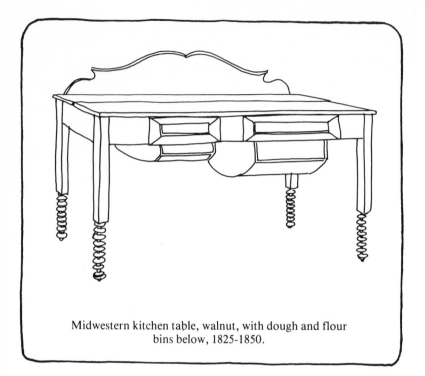

Midwestern kitchen table, walnut, with dough and flour
bins below, 1825-1850.

found hard to compete with, and many of these craftsmen went to work in the furniture factories. A similar fate befell many black-smiths, who were forced to give up their own businesses and begin doing piece work in foundries that at first produced cast-iron steps, railings, street lamps, and fences, and then began to make furniture out of iron.

To staff the growing number of factories, mechanics, woodworkers, and other craftsmen were recruited from Europe. Immigrants from Holland who settled in the Grand Rapids area around midcentury made up a loyal, hard working labor force, and in 1854 the Dutch of Grand Rapids formed an immigration society to help and encourage others from their country to join them. At that time, most of the other furniture workers were New Englanders and New Yorkers. Italian and Scottish woodcarvers were also in demand because, although initial carvings were done by machine, much furniture was still hand finished.

In 1886 a survey at Berkey & Gay, for a time the largest furniture manufacturer in the world, showed that of 255 employees, only 82 were born in this country: 39 were from Michigan, 23 from New York, five from Pennsylvania, four each from Ohio and Indiana, three from Massachusetts, two from New Hampshire, and one each from Kentucky and Illinois. Of the 173 who were foreign-born, more than half, 99, were from Holland, 31 were from Germany, 13 from Canada, nine from Sweden, eight from England, six from Norway and Denmark, three from Ireland, and one each from Wales, Scotland, Russia, and Belgium.

By 1860, there were nine furniture manufacturing establishments in the Grand Rapids area, but in a settlement of 8,000 persons, products such as plaster, lumber, flour and meal, and clothing were more important than furniture. Grand Rapids' days of glory as a furniture center were still ahead.

Chest with drawer pulls in leaf design made in Ontario, mid-19th c.

Grand Rapids and Beyond

In spite of a depression in the late 1850s and the Civil War in the 1860s, the business of Grand Rapids furnituremakers increased tenfold between 1860 and 1870, and another sixfold between 1870 and 1880. In 1865, Comstock, Nelson and Company, using steam-driven machinery, boasted that they turned out "an immense amount" of goods, selling in the "East, West, North and South, from the extreme limits of this state to the western boundaries of Iowa and Minnesota." In 1873, Berkey Brothers and Gay claimed to have shipped about $300,000 worth of furniture to New York, Pennsylvania, Ohio, Indiana, Illinois, Wisconsin, Iowa, Minnesota, Nebraska, Kansas, Missouri, and Colorado.

In 1879 the Grand Rapids Chair Company began producing chairs that met with a "ready sale," according to company records. But the firm did not have an easy time of it. At first, the company had difficulty getting enough workers. Women to weave cane seats were particularly needed. Some of this work was done in homes, where the children helped, and the company offered to deliver supplies to workers at home in any part of the city. It was also difficult to compete with those chair manufacturers who used prison labor to produce cheap chairs. The nationwide financial panic of 1873 did not help matters either, and Grand Rapids furniture companies came and went with some frequency. One Grand Rapids manufacturer said that "Canada saved us from bankruptcy. It was the only market of importance for our goods for which we were promptly paid in real money."

The selling practices of the Grand Rapids furniture companies constitute another interesting chapter in the history of the industry. By the early 1860s, traveling salesmen for Grand Rapids furniture had made their appearance. At first, they carried around small models of their products as samples. They also made rough sketches to show to potential customers. Elias Matter, a Grand Rapids manufacturer, is credited with introducing the use of photographs in 1862. It is said that he got the idea from a salesman for baby carriages whom he met in Jackson, Michigan. The first illustrated catalog was produced by William Widdicomb in 1877. The illustrations were cut on wood and then printed on heavy paper.

Another early selling practice was the use of chartered railroad cars that a salesman, or the manufacturer himself, accompanied from town to town, selling furniture or taking orders from side tracks.

More common, though, were those who traveled from town to town as passengers on regular trains. These salesmen were fiercely competitive, and because the first person to reach a town got the order, trips often turned into races. Usually there was only one train a day through an area, so a salesman could make only one town a day, unless he could catch a ride on a freight.

By the early 1860s, the firm of C.C. Comstock had opened branch stores in Peoria and St. Louis. As this became a more common practice, Grand Rapids manufacturers began leasing display space in large eastern cities. But the greatest change in selling methods came in the 1870s, when buyers for furniture stores began coming to Grand Rapids. From this practice evolved the semiannual (January and July) Grand Rapids furniture markets.

The salesman's life was a hard one, even as late as 1893. Frank Ransom recounts the following story of an adventure of that year in his book *The City Built on Wood*. Two salesmen from competing Grand Rapids companies started out their trip in Milwaukee, then turned northward along the western shore of Lake Michigan. It was a poor year for sales there, and the two decided to leave Wisconsin and take the train for Minneapolis. In the middle of a rainy night they had to change trains and were forced to get off. They helped one another out, burdened by two bags, two sample cases, a suitcase, and a small steamer trunk. The pair found the country station locked and decided to spend the rest of the night in the nearest town, so they hailed the driver of a passing horse and wagon, who refused to take them into town, but it was only a mile and a half on the foot path, he said. The men started on their way, carrying the steamer trunk between them, piled with bags. On a footbridge over a muddy creek, one of them, who was something of a dandy, slipped, and fell—with all the baggage —into the stream. It was a "wet, bedraggled, and muddy pair," Ransom writes, that finally caught the Minneapolis train.

In 1876 the United States celebrated its 100th birthday with the

Philadelphia Centennial Exposition. Three Grand Rapids furniture companies (Berkey and Gay, Nelson-Matter, and Phoenix Furniture) exhibited at the Centennial, and all three won medals. Although the Berkey and Gay bedroom suit was large and heavily carved, the bedstead shown by Nelson-Matter was even more elaborately decorated. It was a massive affair of oak. The head and foot displayed numerous statuettes, including Christopher Columbus, George Washington, Columbia, and Johann Guttenberg. Washington had the place of honor at the center of the headboard, and Columbia was at the foot. Atop the structure was a huge wooden eagle with spread wings. It was, after all, the national centennial.

The *New York Tribune, St. Louis Globe,* and *Chicago Journal* wrote very critically of the American furniture at the Centennial, while praising the English products, especially those of the English architect Charles Eastlake, whose Tudor designs American manufacturers tried to adapt for the next decade. The American pieces at the Centennial were condemned for lack of taste, artistic appeal, and definite design.

After the Centennial, business picked up again for Grand Rapids furnituremakers. Not until the next decade would European markets become important to Grand Rapids firms, but people in all of the United States, Cuba, Puerto Rico, Hawaii, South America, the Philippines, and, of course, Canada were already buying furniture made in Grand Rapids.

Although in 1888 the Board of Trade in Grand Rapids forecast that the supply of hardwood seemed almost inexhaustible and there would be enough lumber in Michigan for the needs of the next 100 years, a decade later Grand Rapids manufacturers were looking far afield for raw materials. Hence, in 1886, the Honduras Lumber Company, which sold mahogany, established an office in Grand Rapids. In 1893, the Widdicomb Furniture Company catalog featured bedroom and dining room furniture of oak, curly birch, bird's-eye maple and mahogany.

For 30 years, Michigan led the nation in lumber production, cutting more than one-half the country's output as late as the 1890s, but after 1900, the Michigan lumber industry dwindled drastically. Mahogany for furniture then came from Cuba, Mexico, Honduras, and Africa. Walnut, which at midcentury had been plentiful in the Midwest, had become scarce and costly, and manufacturers were more sparing with it than with mahogany.

Of the Grand Rapids companies founded before 1870, only three had continuing success. But others were established, and in the 1880s and 1890s, the industry stabilized.

In 1893, the year of the Columbian Exposition in Chicago, it was reported that in Grand Rapids there were 62 firms associated with the furniture industry, with 9,000 employees and a total worth of more than $9 million. At the semiannual furniture markets in Grand Rapids at the turn of the 20th century, outside as well as local manufacturers exhibited their products. In 1908 there were 200 exhibitors, and many more in the years that followed. The influence of Grand Rapids on the world furniture market (although it never produced more than 10 percent of the nation's annual furniture output) was so great that some firms not located in the city incorporated "Grand Rapids" into their company names, a practice that was later halted by the Federal Trade Commission.

What happened in the Grand Rapids furniture industry was paralleled—not in scope, but at least in the progression of events—in countless other towns in the Midwest. The individual furnituremakers of the early 19th century were gradually supplanted in large degree, although never entirely, by factories, which combined the abilities of machines with the talents of skilled workers to manufacture the many products needed by an expanding population. In Sheboygan, Wisconsin, for example, more than 25 factories came into being in the years following the technological changes of the 1850s.

Chicago, a village of 350 people in the summer of 1833, increased its population tenfold in the two years that followed, and as its rapid growth continued it became a point through which thousands of pioneers passed to the West. The supplies for the burgeoning population also went through the city. But a large portion of Chicago was destroyed in the Great Fire of 1871. Fire, always a special hazard for furniture factories, leveled many Chicago businesses; still, the pioneer spirit seemed only temporarily daunted by the catastrophe. For example, the Thayer and Tobey Furniture Company salesroom at the corner of State and Adams was burned out in the fire. But business was resumed at the factory at Randolph and Jefferson, and, in fact, one day after the fire an order was taken there for furniture for the West Side Sherman House Hotel.

Two years later, a survey of Chicago industry reported that there were 56 furniture factories, four chair factories, and one coffin factory in the city. The survey stated: "There are a few branches of manufacture in the city that have made greater advance within the past few years, both in the number of establishments and in the amount of production of those already established, than that of furniture manufacture." The reputation of Chicago manufacturers, the survey claimed, reached across the continent, and "orders for the entire furniture for hotels and elegant and costly dwellings, from the Pacific coast and from the Territories intervening, are not infrequent." Leading Grand Rapids and Cincinnati manufacturers established branches in Chicago, and often lured away designers who studied in the offices of Chicago architects.

Toward the turn of the century, the mail-order business increased dramatically, and much inexpensive furniture was sold through catalogs like those of Montgomery Ward, Sears, Roebuck, John M. Smyth, and Spiegel, May, Stern. (The Chicago Public Library has a complete file of Sears, Roebuck catalogs from 1893 on, a source that is valuable for researchers, dealers, and collectors of furniture produced in those years.)

As machines and factory operations improved, furniture could be made faster and more economically. Also, the population was growing and more Americans were buying more items. According to John Maass in *The Gingerbread Age*, a fashionable Victorian living room was crammed with the following: floral carpets, large-figured wallpaper, overstuffed chairs, tufted ottomans, marble-topped tables, upholstered settees and chairs, potted plants, bronzed statuary, plaster figurines, wax flowers under glass domes, shellwork, beadwork, fringed cushions, gilt-framed pictures, and souvenirs and bric-a-brac on fretwork brackets and tiered whatnots. There probably also were a piano, a bookcase, and a few lamps. And, at the windows, five layers of protection—shutters, blinds, muslin curtains, velvet draperies, and tasseled valances. No wonder the factories were hard-put to keep up with the demand of their products.

After the turn of the century, Grand Rapids dwindled in influence and production. Chicago became the Midwest furniture marketing center, as well as the center for the mail-order business, which was supplied chiefly by factories in Illinois and Indiana. Grand Rapids, however, with its tradition of 100 years of fine furniture making, continued to produce quality furniture, which would work against the Grand Rapids furniture community in the Depression of the 1930s. Because of the luxury character of its product, the furniture industry there suffered a greater loss of business than did most others, although during this period came the first major change in transportation since the railroad entered town—the shipment of uncrated furniture by truck. The furniture makers had only partly recovered when World War II began, and then they were seriously hampered by the restrictions on the use of raw products. An upsurge in business after the war and concurrent modernization of factory and sales methods somewhat revitalized furniture making in Grand Rapids.

In 1937 the city celebrated the 100th anniversary of the establishment of Deacon Haldane's furniture shop, and soon after, to keep alive the tradition of Grand Rapids furniture, the community established the Grand Rapids Public Museum, where collectors can, today, see some of the noteworthy products of the industry from past years.

Across the international border, in Ontario, the furniture industry moved along much as it did in the States. During the first 50 years of the 19th century, furniture was handmade everywhere in Ontario, by handymen or by cabinetmakers. The first settlers were either Loyalists, who emigrated to Canada from the American colonies as a result of the Revolutionary War, or Old Country immigrants. The Loyalists' lands and houses had been confiscated by the brand new government of the United States, and so they arrived in Canada with very few possessions. The fortunate ones brought tools with which they set to work to construct shelter and simple furniture for themselves and their families.

Those Old Country immigrants who tried to bring some furniture with them, in spite of advice to the contrary, often found that it arrived broken, or, at best, that it cost them more to bring it over than to have bought new furniture in Ontario. Wood was cheap and plentiful in the province, and essential furniture such as chairs, tables, and bedsteads was always offered for sale by local woodworkers, who also made chests, cupboards, desks, and coffins. Some woodworkers made and imported only chairs. Variations of American Windsor and English slat-back chairs were the common styles of the early 19th century. Beds, cupboards, and cabinets followed simplified Sheraton and Hepplewhite designs.

Gradually some of the early provincial woodworkers developed their businesses and became full-fledged cabinetmakers. Shops were also established by cabinetmakers from the States who were attracted to Canada because the land was cheap—or free. After 1825, settlers in Ontario bought furniture from below the border as well as from local cabinetmakers. And those who could afford it imported furniture from the Old Country.

For 30 years after 1815, furniture made in Ontario showed an equal influence from England and America in provincial versions of the English Regency, Sheraton, and Hepplewhite styles, and the new American Empire designs. English-made furniture was most often mahogany with brass knobs and pulls. Canadian-made furniture was usually walnut, cherry, or maple, with wooden pulls. Some Quebec-made furniture was brought into Ontario, but it was made, by and large, in shops run by Englishmen, so it showed little French influence.

At midcentury, the Ontario furniture industry was changing, producing mostly inexpensive factory-made furniture rather than homemade items. New techniques, machines, and steam power were turned to making Canadian versions of the styles also popular in the States: Gothic, Elizabethan, Renaissance, and French antique (Louis XIV revival) and Rococo (Louis XV). Elizabethan designs became the commoners' spool-turned furniture, in walnut, maple, and birch, and after 1850, cottage furniture was manufactured in Ontario as it was in the States. Enameled bedroom sets made of a soft wood such as pine, decorated with painted fruit and flowers, were sold for about $25 on both sides of the border.

As the century progressed and Ontario residents became more prosperous, they built bigger houses and bought more furniture. Furniture purchases were made locally—from dealers who sold furniture made both in the States and in the province and from local cabinetmakers. Mail-order shopping did not become popular until the turn of the century.

Interest in collecting old furniture has been increasing during the past 20 years in Ontario and the Midwest. Furniture is, after all, visible, tangible evidence of history, and it is to be hoped that dealers and collectors alike will help preserve these links, sometimes homey, sometimes elegant, with our mutual past.

Early Victorian Furniture

In this and the following two chapters, we will survey trends and trend-makers that affected furniture design and manufacture in the Midwest. Until the 19th century (and, indeed, in some cases, long after that) Americans looked to England and France for styles in architecture and furniture. Before discussing the styles of the Victorian period, let's go back a bit and look briefly at early American furniture.

The hardships of life in the early days of the American colonies were such that only the most utilitarian furniture was made. Wealthy families were able to bring a few pieces with them from England, and some furniture was imported after the colonists settled here, but in the average colonial home furniture consisted of beds, chairs, tables, and chests made from local woods, either by the owners themselves or by local cabinetmakers. This primitive 17th century furniture is usually called Puritan. Its characteristics were simplicity, bulkiness, and good proportions. The wood was often oak, which is difficult to carve, but sturdy.

As the colonies increased in population, so too did the number of furnituremakers. Guilds formed in many towns, and the industry depended on the apprenticeship system. Itinerant joiners went from town to town. In the South, slaves were trained in carpentry and cabinetmaking, and they produced furniture in plantation workshops. Some of these early craftsmen were chairmakers only. Others were trained as turners, woodcarvers, and upholsterers.

At the turn of the 18th century, the William and Mary style was popular. This furniture was bulky, had baroque lines and ball or bun feet. Innovations such as highboy and lowboy chests, gateleg tables, and cabriole (curved) legs appeared.

It was during this period that regional differences in American furniture were most apparent. In England, there were fewer variations

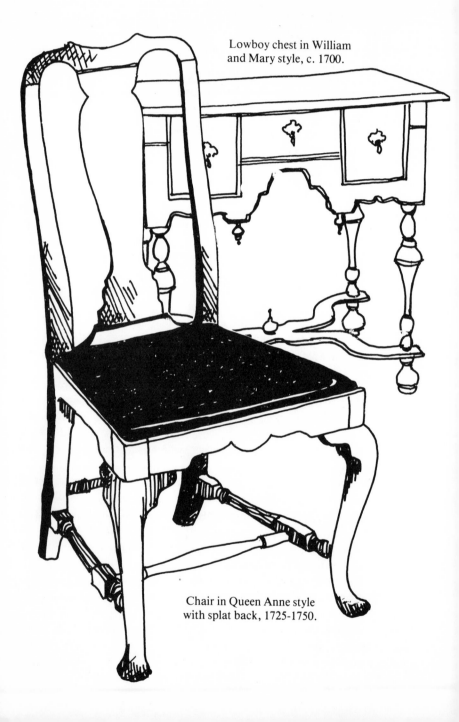

Lowboy chest in William
and Mary style, c. 1700.

Chair in Queen Anne style
with splat back, 1725-1750.

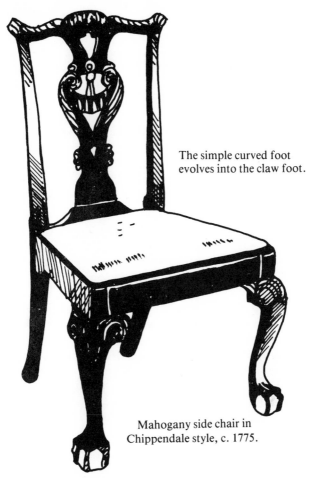

The simple curved foot evolves into the claw foot.

Mahogany side chair in Chippendale style, c. 1775.

because there was only one furniture center, London. But in the colonies, several cities along the Atlantic seaboard were centers of style for their particular regions. Today, experts can tell by looking at an 18th century piece whether it was made in New York, Connecticut, Pennsylvania, or South Carolina. But as roads and communication improved during the 18th century, these differences lessened.

Later, in the days of the pioneer West, regional differences were again noticeable in furniture design. California-made furniture had characteristics distinct from, say, Texas. And New Orleans furniture was heavily influenced by the French. But in the Midwest, differences between states were slight. It is therefore practically impossible to tell just by its appearance whether an early 19th century country piece owned by early settlers in Missouri was made there or brought by the family from Kentucky, or elsewhere in a neighboring locality.

One colonial style that was distinctive was the generously proportioned, Dutch-influenced furniture of New York State. The Dutch
were expert furnituremakers, and English and American cabinetmakers were much influenced by ideas from Holland, as well as by
Dutch craftsmen who immigrated to England and the colonies. But
by 1725 the great chests, the wide, deep chairs, and the simple, strong
tables of the patroons had given way to the delicate pad feet and shell
and leaf carving of the Queen Anne style. The heyday of the Queen
Anne style lasted only from about 1725 to 1750, although it is still
used today in reproductions. Toward the end of the period, touches of
what would be Chippendale design crept in. For example, the feet of
the Queen Anne curved legs were sometimes carved into animal claws,
a variation that eventually developed into the claw and ball foot, one
of the most distinguishing features of Chippendale.

As Queen Anne became Chippendale, carving grew more elaborate.
Proportions became heavier, and comfort and solidity were desired
characteristics. Furniture was made mostly of mahogany and walnut,
except in New England, where cherry was favored, but after about 30
years, the pendulum swung again, this time to the fragile elegance of
Hepplewhite and Sheraton. Hepplewhite came slightly earlier, from
about 1785 to 1810. In this furniture style, there was less carving than
in Chippendale. Legs became square and tapered. Veneer, which had
lost favor during the Chippendale period, returned. (It is a widely held
misconception that veneer always signifies inexpensive furniture construction. Veneering has been done for about 300 years and has been
used in some of the most expensive furniture.) Hepplewhite chairs
typically had backs carved in the shapes of shields or hearts.

As furnituremakers acquired machine power, the designs of Thomas Sheraton, an English furnituremaker, became popular. The legs of
this furniture were turned on a lathe, which carved the wood into rods
of different designs, and backs of chairs became square instead of
shield-shaped.

In 1795, when Sheraton and Hepplewhite were both in favor with
those who could afford fine furniture, Duncan Phyfe opened a shop
in New York City. For the next 50 years, he was the most popular
American furnituremaker and designer. His customers were well-to-
do residents of New York, New Jersey, Philadelphia, and the great
Southern plantations. Phyfe's designs carried on the light, delicate appearance of Sheraton and Hepplewhite, but with touches of Greek
and Roman design. In Duncan Phyfe furniture, every line was curved
except the seat. Typical carvings were wheat, leaves, and sheaves of
lightning. The favored wood was mahogany.

Sheraton-style side chair, 1790.
Sheraton backs are
square-shaped. Front legs
are round.

Chair with shield-shaped
back designed by Hepplewhite.
The style was popular
1785-1810. Some Hepplewhite
chairs had heart-shaped backs.

Sheraton and Hepplewhite chairs
are similar in style and date.

The neoclassical furniture styles of the turn of the 18th century melded into what is known as American Empire, usually dated 1815 to 1840. This period marked the beginning of the end for the fine old cabinetmaker. Although some furniture continued to be custom-made, both in large cities and in pioneer country, mass production became more the mode, and furniture became bulkier and heavier to complement the larger homes being built in well-settled areas.

In American Empire furniture, curves sloped downward, and front legs were concave-curved. The gondola chair is a charming, simple design from the period. It was very popular in the Midwest and was generally referred to as a "Grecian chair." Many later ones had bold carving, feet in the shape of fat balls or animal legs and paws, which sometimes, in the more elaborate pieces, had wings.

The hardware of the period was typically a round brass knob, with perhaps an eagle or some other patriotic motif. Later, ring pulls hanging from brass lion heads became popular. Woods became more varied and included mahogany, rosewood, cherry, maple, and softwoods with red stain.

The first indications of an American Victorian style appeared in the 1830s. During this transitional period, the bulky lines of American Empire were retained, but Victorian details such as wavy molding and applied carving were superimposed. Marble tops were sometimes used for tables and chests of drawers, and drawer pulls were typically wooden mushroom-shaped knobs or rosettes of wood or pressed glass. The fashionable bed of the period was the sleigh bed, usually made of mahogany or rosewood, but sometimes of pine or other soft woods.

Commonly made as far west as Wisconsin was a bed that had four high posts, all alike, without a frame for a tester, or canopy. There were low-post beds, too, made for second-story bedrooms with low ceilings and whose head and foot posts were identical. In the South, what is now commonly known as the four-poster bed became popular with those who could afford them. These "plantation beds" had high posts and often a tester over which mosquito netting was draped.

Another typical piece made in the Midwest between 1840 and 1865 was a drop-leaf table with four tapering, turned legs. They were made of black walnut, maple, or fruitwoods such as cherry and butternut.

Duncan Phyfe is credited with having made some of this Early Victorian Transitional furniture, but his era was drawing to a close. His shops in New York shut their doors in 1846 and he died in 1854. An inventory of his household effects listed 16 Victorian pieces out of 110.

Now the Victorian era was truly beginning. As we have mentioned before, Victorian American furniture was made in a wide variety of styles and showed influences from all periods of art history and from all over the world. Victorians loved things that reminded them of antiquity, and they revived and elaborated on several classical styles. They

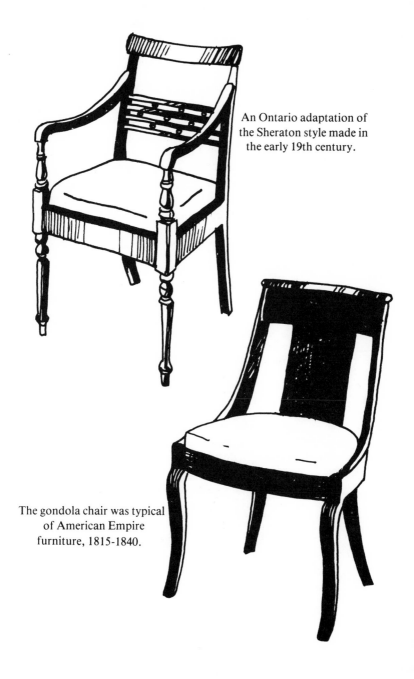

An Ontario adaptation of
the Sheraton style made in
the early 19th century.

The gondola chair was typical
of American Empire
furniture, 1815-1840.

were also intrigued with the exotic. They adopted some items of furniture from the Near East (ottomans, oversized pillows, overstuffed chairs, inlaid tables, hanging brass lamps) and continued to import Oriental rugs and chinaware.

French influence was evident in American revivals of Louis XIV, XV, and XVI styles and in turn-of-the-20th-century Art Nouveau. English designs were translated into Gothic, Elizabethan, and Renaissance Revival styles. The famous (or infamous) Eastlake style of 1875-1885 was adapted from the ideas of an English architect of that name, and the Mission and Golden Oak styles of the turn of the 20th century were what Americans made of the attempts of John Ruskin and William Morris to reform English design. These influences, more simply interpreted, can also be discerned in country furniture, even though we often assume that most of these pieces were made purely for utilitarian purposes and the makers couldn't have known or cared very much about the finer points of design.

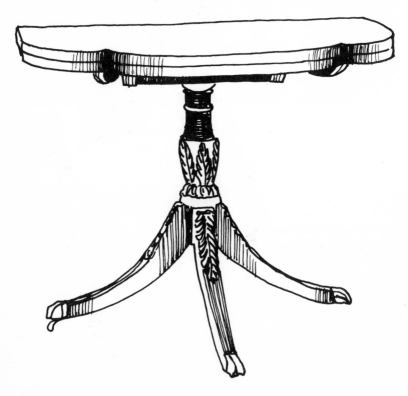

Mahogany table by Duncan Phyfe, c. 1800.

Pedestal table.

Scroll-footed furniture designed by John Hall, 1840.

As Duncan Phyfe passed out of the picture, a Baltimore architect named John Hall was designing a new style of furniture, one that was to flourish between 1840 and 1850. Hall published a book titled *The Cabinet Maker's Assistant*, for which he drew the designs and wrote the text. He has been accused of being an opportunist, because his designs could be made inexpensively with newly available furniture-making machinery. The deep carvings of the American Empire design required laborious work if a cabinetmaker had to use a hand chisel, but Hall's curved furniture could be made with the steam-driven band saw, which was capable of cutting sharp curves in thick pieces of wood.

The result was heavy, scrolled-foot furniture that looked impressive and could be made inexpensively and in large quantities to meet the needs of the country's growing middle class. Mahogany and rosewood veneers were much used in furniture of the Hall design; and sometimes the veneers concealed inferior wood and workmanship. This furniture, called "scroll furniture" in Midwestern advertisements, can still be found in antique shops, a fact that is a testimony to its sturdiness, if not its esthetic excellence. Testy old Duncan Phyfe called it "butcher furniture." If you compare the chunky lines of the scroll furniture with the graceful ones of Phyfe's work, you can see why the old master might so label the Hall products.

Another outstanding feature of this period (variously called Late Empire, Early Victorian, or Transitional Victorian) was the overhanging top drawers in chests and sideboards. In a few years, this feature disappeared, and all drawers were flush.

At the height of the popularity of Hall's designs, another man appeared whose name would become one of the best known in the history of American furniture. John Henry Belter, a German-trained

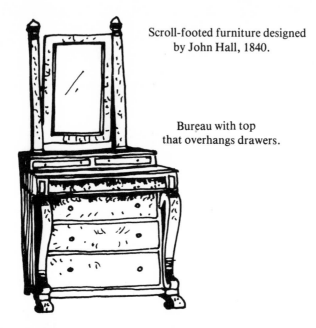

Scroll-footed furniture designed
by John Hall, 1840.

Bureau with top
that overhangs drawers.

mechanic and woodcarver, set up a furniture shop in New York City.
Belter's work could not be criticized for being crude and labeled
"butcher furniture." On the contrary, out of his shop came furniture
that must be among the most elaborately carved in history.

The middle class couldn't afford Belter furniture then, and certainly
can't now. The few pieces of Belter that are sold at auction go for
thousands of dollars and most of it ends up in museums or mansions
that are maintained by dollars the tourists pay to walk through.

Belter's inspiration came from the French rococo furniture of the
Louis XV period. At the time, the style was commonly called "French
antique," but the term has fallen out of use today. The innovations he
developed were heavy, pierced carving and the use of laminated wood,
a product that dropped out of the picture with his passing, not to be
revived until the turn of the 20th century, when it became what we
know as plywood.

Other makers also produced Louis XV revival furniture, although
none quite as elaborate and well-executed as Belter's. It is probably
the best-known Victorian style, epitomized by the balloon-back chair
with slender, curved legs. The tables were marble-topped, oval-
shaped, and supported by tall, curved legs with X-shaped stretchers
(horizontal braces). And the woodworkers indulged themselves with
all types of carving, rose and grape motifs among the most popular.

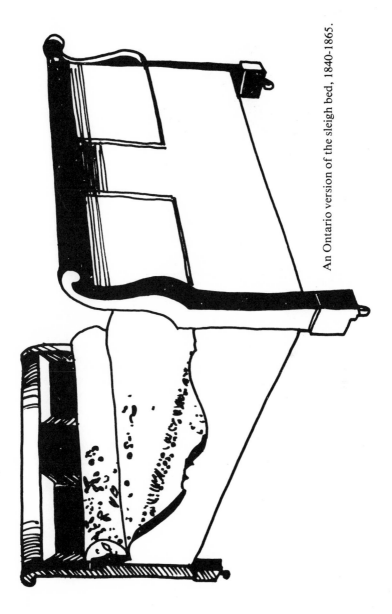

An Ontario version of the sleigh bed, 1840-1865.

Side chair heavily carved in grape and leaf design,
made in John Henry Belter's shop.

During this period the carved-leaf wooden drawer pulls appear; they are commonly seen on pieces in antique shops today. First made around 1840, these pulls continued to be popular for nearly 50 years. The elaborately carved and quaintly named whatnot (or étagère), a piece with open shelves for ornaments, was an invention of the period, as was the upholstered "lady's chair" with low arms. The chair was popular with women because it could gracefully accommodate their hoops and crinoline skirts, while the "gentleman's chair" (with arms) could not. The two were often made in matching pieces.

Another innovation was the manufacture of furniture in matching sets for parlors, dining rooms, bedrooms, and libraries. A full parlor set consisted of a sofa or love seat, a gentleman's chair, a lady's chair, four side chairs, and a center table.

Godey's Lady's Book (the *Woman's Home Companion* of the time) listed the items the editors considered desirable for the well-appointed house of 1850. They were, for the hall, a hat stand with umbrella receptacle and mirror, chairs, and a folding table. Oak was the preferred wood for hall furniture. For the parlor, a sofa and chairs of rosewoodwood, covered in crimson and black satin damask, or, if of mahogany, covered in velvet, plush, or hair. Also *de rigueur* were armchairs upholstered in patterned silk, a "sofa table," oval in shape, and topped with marble (yellow marble cost twice as much as white), an *étagère* in black walnut, and a piano. For the bedroom, a wardrobe, a dressing bureau of black walnut with oval swinging mirrors, a bedstead, and a bedside table. In the dining room, a table, chairs, and sidetables.

Louis XV Revival furniture was made in the major cities of the East —New York, Philadelphia, and Boston—as well as in Cincinnati, and, later, Grand Rapids. As you might suspect, being of French inspiration, it was especially popular in New Orleans, the hub of French-American culture.

An additional point about French revival furniture as exemplarized by Belter. Until this period, quality furniture for sophisticated clients had been made almost exclusively of mahogany and rosewood, both of which had to be imported from the tropics. (One exception was cherry, which found favor in New England.) Now furnituremakers discovered the excellence of the native American black walnut, and much of the furniture of this Mid-Victorian period was made of it. Eventually, of course, black walnut became as scarce as the tropical woods, and then oak became more popular.

By 1850, the circular saw had come into common use. The bandsaw was invented in 1850, and soon fret-cutting machinery became avail-

Gothic Revival side chair with typical arch design, c. 1840.

able, which was a big help. But even in factories where the rough cutting and shaping was executed by machine, finishing continued to be done by hand.

During these midcentury years, American furniture designers and manufacturers began to come into their own. No longer did all the really expensive pieces come from England and France. Belter's furniture, though in questionable taste, was of excellent construction and workmanship. And there were still master craftsmen in custom furniture shops. But, just as in England, the middle class in America was increasing in size and power, and their needs had to be met. Furniture-makers were ready and willing, and during this period factories blossomed throughout the settled areas of the United States and Canada, even in the Midwest.

The popular balloon-back chair, walnut.

Mid-Victorian Furniture

Spool furniture was the first style to be consistently factory-made in America. It was popular between 1850 and 1880, although some pieces were made in small shops at the beginning of the century, and it was manufactured in Massachusetts, Vermont, Maine, Ohio, and by the Sheboygan (Wisconsin) Chair Company as late as 1890. Made for the middle class, spool furniture is sometimes classified as "country furniture." Whatever its classification, it is highly prized today.

With some diligence, you can find beds, towel racks, small tables, and washstands in the spool furniture design. The most well-known piece was, and still is, the Jenny Lind bed, so-called because the famous Swedish singer slept in a bed of that style during a tour of the United States. Spool furniture got its name from its turnings, which were usually spool-shaped, but knob, sausage, spiral, bobbin, vase, and ring forms were also used. The turnings were produced in long pieces, and the cabinetmaker would cut off the lengths needed for the piece he was making. Origins of spool furniture can be traced to Flemish furniture of the 17th century. Elizabethan influences can also be detected.

The period around 1850 must have been particularly inspirational, because several other, widely varying, furniture styles also began to appear then. Around 1845 there was a brief revival of the Elizabethan style. Its chief characteristic was the spiral turning, from which the spool furniture design probably evolved.

And there were other revivals of medieval designs. For a 35-year period, beginning about 1830, architects who designed official, academic, or ecclesiastical buildings in the Gothic style dictated that the Gothic style should also be used for the furniture in those buildings. And some Gothic furniture was custom-made for mansions of the day. These pieces were large, formal, and they were certainly not popular with the general public—perhaps because, for the most part,

43

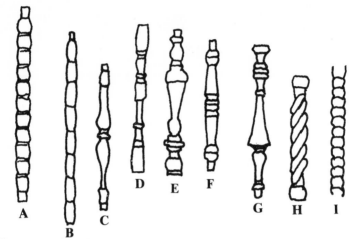

Some examples of turnings: (a) ball and ring) (b) sausage; (c) vase and ring,
(d) baluster: (e) cup; (f) spindle; (g) trumpet; (h) spiral; (i) spool.

they were uncomfortable. The Gothic style was rarely attempted by cabinetmakers in small towns, and you won't see it much in antique shops, but the characteristic pointed arched panel does show up occasionally in furniture not otherwise in the grand Gothic manner.

Victorian furniture in the Renaissance Revival style also has a grand-mansion appearance and proportion. Its lines were adapted from Renaissance architecture: heavy and straight, with pediments (ornamental tops) and carved medallions. Massive sideboards, large round extension tables, small marble-topped tables, carved beds with tall headboards, and bureaus with marble tops and mirrors were typical Renaissance pieces. They were usually made of black walnut or mahogany and were produced in quantity by the quality factories in Grand Rapids.

The influence of Renaissance Revival may also be seen in many pieces of the period that were copies of more expensive furniture. Chests of drawers with leaf-carved wooden handles (sometimes with mirrors and marble tops) that are common in Midwestern shops today were copies of chests made for the rich folks. The Renaissance Revival style was popular almost until the end of the century. By that time, the obsession for pediments had reached the point of absurdity. (A small, inexpensive oak parlor table in our living room has eight pediments, and its design is not all that unusual.)

Spool bed, often made
of maple, 1850-1880.

Cottage-style dresser with painted
fruit and flower decorations,
popular during the
last half of the 19th

Maple washstand with towel
racks at sides, Ontario, c. 1850.

Probably most important to the average collector of Victorian furniture today is the country furniture of the period. It is available and relatively inexpensive, and its medium size makes it appropriate for use in today's homes and apartments.

Generally included in the country furniture category are spool furniture (previously discussed in this chapter), utilitarian kitchen pieces (see Chapter 8), simple furniture with various design influences made by local craftsmen and in factories (see Chapters 7 and 8), and cottage furniture. Cottage furniture was made in factories from 1850 to 1890. It was usually painted white, gray, lilac, or blue, sometimes with flowers or other designs. Bedroom sets were the most popular groups. A slight French Empire influence can be seen in some pieces, but tables, chairs, and towel racks have spool turnings. When found with the original paint, cottage furniture is prized. Most often, however, it

Renaissance Revival chair made in Grand Rapids, c. 1875.

has been painted several times, and it is nearly impossible to remove only the top layers to get down to the original paint.

A few particular types of chairs were commonly used throughout the Victorian period, so much so, in fact, that they were considered appropriate in all but the most formal mansions. These were the Windsor, the ladderback, the "fancy" (Hitchcock) chair, and the rocker, one of the few uniquely American furniture inventions.

Windsor chairs have been made since the 15th century, when Windsor, England, was an important city. Wheelwrights or wagonwrights made the first Windsor chairs, shaping the spindles for the backs with the same tools they used to make wheel spokes. Windsors in pioneer America had seats shaped with hand tools. The wood was a soft variety without knots, and the face of the seat was hollowed out of a plank two inches thick. The legs and stretchers were then attached through holes in the seat and secured with wooden wedges and/or glue. Both the seat and legs were made from green wood, which shrank as it dried out and kept the legs in place.

Firehouse-style Windsor,
Ontario, mid-19th c.

Windsor made by
Deacon Haldane in
Grand Rapids, c. 1840.

Painted Windsor chair made
in Ontario between 1825-1840.

The more spindles there are in the back of a Windsor (as many as 11), the earlier the chair. There were, and still are, since Windsors are still being made, several kinds of turnings and backs. They come, for example, in low, comb, fan, hoop, bow, and rod varieties. Chairmakers often used several different kinds of wood in a chair, and they therefore painted them so the chairs would present a uniform appearance. Common colors were dark green, red, black, yellow, and white. So popular were chairs of Windsor design that they were used in almost every sitting situation—from the legislative houses of the state of Wisconsin to taverns to the simplest pioneer kitchen.

Ladderback (or slatback) straight chairs originated in England in the 1600s and have been made ever since. They were popular with country chairmakers because the legs did not have to be turned, although most were. Seats of early ladderbacks were of rawhide, rush, splint, or, in the case of the Shaker chairs, woven tape, and the joiners who made the early ladderback chairs did not use nails. As with the Windsors, the legs were made of unseasoned wood and the rungs (or stretchers) of seasoned wood, so that when the unseasoned wood dried out and shrank, it gripped the seasoned rungs tightly.

The so-called "fancy chair" of Victorian times was an adaptation of the Sheraton style. It was intended not only to sit on, but to be admired as a thing of beauty. Fancy chairs, first made in the East, were, by midcentury, also being turned out in quantity by chairmakers in the Midwest. Country chairmakers in the first quarter of the century made rush seats. Later, seats were made of cane, and, by the 1850s, they were of wood.

Early fancy chairs were expensive, but eventually they came within the price range of almost everyone. They were used in dining rooms, parlors, bedrooms, bars, and hotels. And they were so popular on steamboats that in some areas they were called "steamboat fancies."

Lambert Hitchcock of Connecticut was the best-known fancy-chairmaker. By 1821 he was making chairs in a water-power driven shop in what is now Riverton, Connecticut. At first he made chair parts for shipment to Charleston, South Carolina, but he soon turned to producing complete chairs. The Hitchcock type of chair can still be found at moderate prices in the Midwest, evidence enough of the fact that they were produced in quantity. The backs of fancy chairs were decorated with handpainted or stencil drawings. Although most chairs made by the Hitchcock factory were painted black, other chairmakers used other colors, similar to those of the painted Windsor chairs.

It's still argued whether or not Benjamin Franklin invented the rocking chair. In any case, he owned one, and they were first used in

"Fancy" chair showing
Sheraton influence, decorated
with stenciling, 1830-1890.

Country-made slatback
chair, Midwest, early 19th c.
The tapered-bottom legs
are a Midwestern characteristic.

An Ontario adaptation
of the Windsor, an arrowback
design in maple with basswood
seat, mid-19th c.

Two rocking chairs of the late 19th c.

Gooseneck rocker (also called
a Lincoln rocker because
the President owned one)
made about 1860.

Late Victorian platform rocker.

Philadelphia about 1770. They were not acceptable in formal rooms until almost a hundred years later, but in the meantime they became very popular in other parts of the house. They were fairly common in pioneer houses, and in some cases when a family wanted a rocker, they converted a straight chair by cutting off the legs a bit and adding rockers.

Very early rocking chairs (before 1825) had short, stubby rockers that extended equal distances beyond the front and rear legs. The rule is that the greater the distance the rockers extend in the rear, the later the chair. You probably won't see rocking chairs old enough to have short rear rockers except in museums. Some rocking chairs made entirely of maple were left unpainted. But most were made of several different kinds of wood—the seat of one wood, other parts of other woods—and were painted.

Boston and Salem rockers both came into favor about 1840, and they remained popular for some 50 years. They differ in that the Salem rocker has a flat seat while the Boston rocker has a seat that is rolled—it curves downward in the front. The back of the Boston rocker is higher than that of the Salem. Early Boston rockers frequently had stenciled designs on the back.

Late Victorian rockers made of oak often have a design pressed into the wood of the back, and they are generally called "pressed-back" rockers. The Sleepy Hollow rocker (so-called because it was an adaptation of Washington Irving's favorite chair) was popular in the Midwest between 1850 and 1870. It was overstuffed, curved, and comfortable. Another type of rocking chair, the Lincoln rocker, was named for the chair in which President Lincoln was sitting when he was shot.

After 1870, a variety of platform rockers were produced. These exemplified the Victorian trait of mechanical inventiveness—the base remained stationary while the chair rocked on a spring mechanism. A platform rocker had two principal advantages: it didn't move from place to place when a person rocked in it, and it didn't wear out the carpet underneath as fast as a traditional rocker.

In 1875, the United States celebrated its 100th birthday. The following year, Philadelphia hosted a world's fair, the Centennial Exposition, where huge crowds of people were attracted by moving models of new machines such as the web printing press, the self-binding reapers, the typewriter, and the telephone.

Industrialization and mechanization were strong influences on Victorian furnituremakers. As the century progressed, more and more furniture was made by machine, and sometimes, unfortunately, the design of the pieces depended upon the capabilities of the machinery

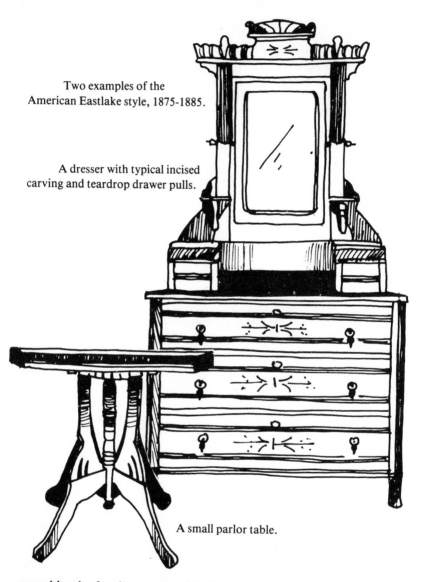

Two examples of the
American Eastlake style, 1875-1885.

A dresser with typical incised
carving and teardrop drawer pulls.

A small parlor table.

owned by the furnituremaker. Mechanical innovations crept into furniture design, resulting in such things as platform rockers, tilting
chairs, beds that pulled out of bookcases, and steamer trunks that
converted to life rafts. New industrial processes also promoted the use
of materials other than wood for furniture, and we still find in antique
shops furnishings from the Victorian era of iron, wire, rattan, gutta
percha, and papier mache.

The furniture that was the real sensation of the 1876 Centennial Exposition was the sturdy oak designs of an English architect, Charles L. Eastlake. Concerned about the lack of good taste in the homes of the new English mercantile rich, Eastlake rebelled against the excessively curved French rococo revival furniture that was popular at the time.

His original designs had the straight lines of the English Jacobean period. In his book, first published in 1868, *Hints on Household Taste*, Eastlake championed solid wood. "Never buy veneered work of any kind," he advised, pointing out that the natural grain of wood is itself an ornamental feature, a fact that he was not the first nor the last furniture designer to notice. "But," he went on (and that was where he made his mistake), "where an effect of greater richness is aimed at, two legitimate modes of decoration are available for wood, carving and marquetry or inlaid work."

Eastlake's pompous pronouncements were published in the United States in 1872, and as we have noted, his designs were admired in Philadelphia four years later. American furniture manufacturers seized upon the new straight-line style and adapted it to fit their capabilities. The result was furniture with basic rectangular shape, decorated with machine-incised designs and glued-on veneer panels. Drawer pulls of the black teardrop design were used, and with luck can still be found on good pieces made during the 1875-1885 period when Eastlake was most popular.

American Eastlake furniture (though of English design, Eastlake was never manufactured in England) has been condemned as being shoddily made and atrociously designed, but the better quality pieces, of oak or walnut, command good prices today, and the cheap ones are, if nothing else, sturdy—as their age attests.

Good and bad examples of the Eastlake style can easily be found in antique shops of the Midwest.

Still another, entirely different, type of furniture exhibited at the Philadelphia Centennial Exposition in 1876 was that of the Shakers. Ann Lee, an English religious visionary, emigrated to New York in 1774 with seven followers, determined to form a colony of believers. By 1850, there were 18 Shaker colonies, including settlements as far west as Ohio, Kentucky, and Indiana, but their populations dwindled after the Civil War.

The western Shaker colonies were dissolved early in this century, and the furniture was disposed of at that time. Although rare and expensive, genuine Shaker pieces can still be found around the countryside, or at least seen in museums. The influence of Shaker designs can be detected in other furniture of that period—and, in fact, in furniture

Chest of drawers,
butternut, 1827.

Trestle table, walnut.

Two examples of Shaker craftsmanship, Midwest.

being made today. The Shakers believed that their furniture was designed by the angels, and they tried to make it perfect. One of their
considerations when making a chair was that an angel might come and
sit upon it. To the honest, hardworking Shakers, inferior workmanship, unnecessary turnings, applied decoration, veneers, and carvings
were wasteful, distracting, and imperfect. Function and simplicity
were the characteristics they considered important.

Shaker furniture is finely proportioned. Legs are thin and tapering.
Chair backs have simple slats. At first the seats were rush, but later
they were made of woven tape. Acorn-shaped finials (the turned
knobs at the ends of the the upright members of chair backs) were
typical.

Shakers were little influenced by changing styles in the world
outside their settlements, and so Shaker designs evolved slowly. Furniture made by western Shakers was heavier and more severe than that
made by their Eastern counterparts, and some superfluous turnings
appear in the Midwestern pieces. In the East, Shakers made furniture
of pine, maple, cherry, birch, and butternut. In the Midwest, favored
woods were poplar and black walnut, with some pine, butternut, and
cherry.

Two Shaker rockers, showing
differences in Eastern
and Midwestern designs.

Eastern-style Shaker rocker with
tape back and seat and delicately
carved arms and finials.

A Shaker rocker made in Kentucky,
showing generally heavier design.

Late Victorian Furniture

Although Victorian furniture was made primarily of wood, furniture manufacturers were eager to use other materials as well.

A story is told of Cyrus Wakefield, a young man who operated a grocery store in Boston with his brother in 1844. One day he stood on the wharf watching the unloading of a vessel from the Far East. A stevedore threw a small bundle of rattan over the rail. Wakefield asked about it and was told it had little value. Rattan, a palm, was used as ballast for the ship. Wakefield bought the bundle and carried it to his grocery store. From this happenstance grew the Wakefield Rattan Company, which used the pith of the reed to make the bodies of chairs and the outside to make chair seats. The enterprise grew, and the Heywood-Wakefield Company eventually came to consider itself the "first and foremost" reed and cane furniture company in the country—at least that's what its advertisements claimed in 1926.

Wicker (a term used here to include all woven furniture—reed, rattan, willow, and fiber) was in its heyday in the 1890s, but continued to be very popular as porch or summer home furniture for another 30 years. At the height of its popularity, wicker was used for tables, beds, chairs, settees, rockers, desks, even phonographs. Bamboo (or "simulated bamboo"—wooden furniture turned to look like bamboo) was also popular throughout the same period.

Another material the Victorians were fond of using for furniture was cast iron. As early as the 1830s cast-iron columns, grilles, and balconies were being produced in the Midwest, and soon afterwards garden furniture was made by the cast-iron method (as opposed to wrought iron). Within the following 25 years, cast-iron was used for a variety of articles, including hatracks, tables, beds, and mirrors. Only beds retained great popularity. In turn-of-the-century furniture catalogs, iron beds were advertised as more desirable than wooden ones because they were "more sanitary."

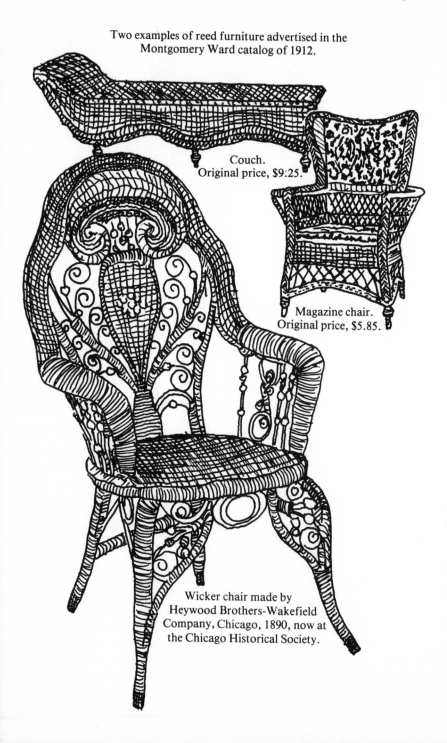

Two examples of reed furniture advertised in the
Montgomery Ward catalog of 1912.

Couch.
Original price, $9.25.

Magazine chair.
Original price, $5.85.

Wicker chair made by
Heywood Brothers-Wakefield
Company, Chicago, 1890, now at
the Chicago Historical Society.

It's true that iron beds were used in many hospitals, but it's difficult to say whether that was so because they were actually more sanitary—or whether the public assumed they were more sanitary because they were used in hospitals.

Also on medical advice, twin beds were introduced in the 1890s and were accepted with enthusiasm by at least part of the population. Presumably sleeping alone was considered a deterrent to the spread of disease.

Iron was also combined with brass in beds, a combination that could be very attractive and was about half as expensive as an all-brass bed—two advantages that still hold true.

Nevertheless, all-brass beds were within the reach of the average person. In 1912, the Montgomery Ward catalog proclaimed, "To own a brass bed is every woman's proper ambition," and to prove it offered brass beds for $10 to $20. They were guaranteed for 10 years.

Small pieces of Victorian furniture were also made of papier mache and lacquer. Most of them were manufactured in England and in the cities of the Eastern seaboard. Some eventually made their way westward, and they turn up occasionally in antique shops.

To make papier mache, a mixture of vegetable matter, paper, and hemp was pressed into sheets upon an iron mold. Several layers were pressed together, pasted, and dried in an oven, then waterproofed and finished with several coats of shiny varnish. Papier mache pieces were decorated by painting and by inlaid designs of pearl and real or artificial gems. Small tables, side chairs, boxes, mirrors, and the like were the most popular papier mache and lacquer pieces.

Another innovation in furniture that captured the fancy of American Victorians was designs from the Near East. Furniture and accessories from the Near East were exhibited at the Centennial Exposition, and for years after that, many well-to-do homes had "Turkish cozy corners." These were small rooms or parts of rooms that were furnished with items from, or inspired by, the Near East and India. And the boxlike, upholstery-covered, fringed chairs and divans in the Near Eastern style of this period were the ancestors of our present-day overstuffed furniture. The ottoman (a round sofa with a raised section in the middle), the small inlaid "Damascus" table, and hanging pierced metal lamps were also introduced at this time. Oriental motifs in architecture, wallpaper, and fabrics that appeared during the late 19th century are further evidence of the Victorian interest in the Near East, an interest that was partly inspired by the opening of the Suez Canal, in 1869.

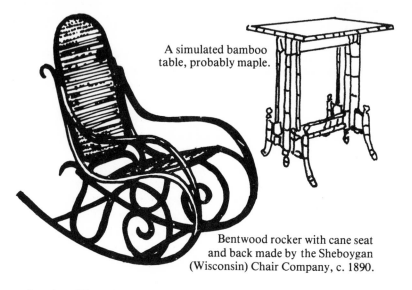

A simulated bamboo table, probably maple.

Bentwood rocker with cane seat and back made by the Sheboygan (Wisconsin) Chair Company, c. 1890.

Another Victorian design that is still quite popular today is the bentwood furniture originated in Vienna by Michael Thonet. First made in 1840, bentwood furniture is still being manufactured around the world in styles little different from Thonet's original ideas. Pieces of wood (originally birch, later, other woods) were steamed and bent, the result being a simple design that was lightweight but strong. Thonet's designs and methods were widely copied. Bentwood furniture parts were made in large quantities in factories and then shipped unassembled to dealers, who put them together with screws. Original Thonets still occasionally turn up in Midwestern shops. They are marked on the bottom with his name.

One of the strangest Victorian products was horn, or trophy, furniture. Horns of buffalos and steers were used to make the backs, legs, and arms of chairs, settees, and tables. The seats were most often upholstered in leather, but velvets and damasks were also used. Other items, such as hatracks, were occasionally made of horns, and there were also umbrella stands made of elephant legs and inkwells of rhinoceros feet.

This fad fit in with Teddy Roosevelt's interests perfectly, and he used the zoological motif in decorating his Long Island home. Probably his own popularity was responsible for perpetuating the interest in horn furniture, an aberration that lasted about 50 years, until the pre-World War I period. Recently I saw a steerhorn chair, upholstered in green damask and heavily fringed, for sale in a Richmond, Illinois, shop for $500.

By the end of the 19th century, the Victorian penchant for diversity had reached its zenith. American furniture styles included Gothic, French rococo, Renaissance Revival, Eastlake, Near Eastern, and Far Eastern, and were made of wood, metal, papier mache, wicker, and horns.

The stage was set for a revolutionary, unifying influence, and onto that stage strode Gustav Stickley. One of 11 children, Stickley was born in Osceola, Wisconsin, in 1857. His father, a stonemason and farmer, abandoned his family in the 1870s, and his mother was forced to take her children east to Pennsylvania where her brother operated a small chair factory. Gustav, then about 15 or 16, left school in the eighth grade and, to make money for his family, hauled logs at night to the lumber mill.

Even at that age, Gustav loved wood. Eventually, he and all five of his brothers became furniture manufacturers. By the time Stickley was 21, he was foreman and manager of his uncle's factory, the Brandt Chair Company. Then, he and two of his brothers opened a furniture store in Binghamton, Pennsylvania, where they sold inexpensive, machine-made furniture in the 1880s.

But in 1886 Gustav Stickley began producing handcrafted furniture in a new style—plain, solid oak furniture with strong, straight lines, often with leather cushions or table tops.

"Oak furniture that shows plainly what it is and in which the design and construction harmonize with the wood will in time become very valuable," Stickley wrote prophetically. His designs, revolutionary for the time, show the influence of the Japanese style as well as the simple forms of the Shakers. This furniture of Stickley's, which he called "Craftsman," is now regarded as the first "modern" furniture. After he exhibited it at the Grand Rapids furniture market in 1900, it became widely popular and widely imitated. Imitators called their products "Mission," "Hand-Craft," "Arts and Crafts," and "Quaint." Now the style is generally referred to as Mission, because copiers of Stickley's designs claimed they were adapted from the Indian-made furniture in the Spanish mission of the American West. Stickley never said that was where his ideas came from, but he was a serious student of primitive peoples and cultures, so it is possible that his inspiration came from the original mission furniture.

Gustav Stickley was at the height of his glory in 1913. Two years later, he was bankrupt. In the meantime he had opened the Craftsman

Workshops in New York State, founded *The Craftsman* magazine, and built the 12-story Craftsman building in New York City, which housed a lecture hall, a library, a homebuilders' exhibit, furniture, and textiles.

A few years later, Stickley, who never shook off his Wisconsin pioneer farm background, returned to Kenosha as a consultant to a furniture factory. He wasn't very successful in that capacity either, and lived in relative obscurity until his death in 1942.

Deliberately inexpensive and primitive, Mission furniture was made and sold in great quantities during the turn-of-the-century period. Among Stickley's "unscrupulous imitators" (his phrase) were two of his brothers, who owned Stickley Brothers Company in Grand Rapids. Their 1904 catalog described their furniture as "the extreme protest of the modern artist craftsman against flimsy and faulty construction."

Gustav Stickely's work also influenced the great architect Frank Lloyd Wright, who, although he claimed he hated the Mission style, himself designed furniture with similar straight lines. Both Stickley and Wright were believers in built-in furniture—and what Wright didn't build in, he often screwed to the floor so users wouldn't move it out of place in his carefully designed interiors.

Stickely's Craftsman furniture was part of an arts and crafts movement in America that was a reaction against the ornate, machine-made styles of the time. Arts and crafts proponents believed that artistically designed and made items could and should be used every day. Artistic utilitarianism rather than ornamentation was their ideal. (A revival of that ideal can be seen in our own contemporary arts and crafts movement.) There was a similar trend in England, which also resulted in plain, straight-lined furniture.

Concurrent with the arts and crafts movement was Art Nouveau, a style whose principal form was stylized flowers with trailing tendrils. It was very effective for graphic arts such as posters and illustrations, as well as glassware, pottery, and jewelry, but it did not have much effect on furniture design.

Aubrey Beardsley was the best-known and probably most talented English illustrator in the Art Nouveau style. Tragically, he died at the age of 26. His counterpart in the United States was Will Bradley, a graphic artist who also designed some furniture in the Mission style and added to it Art Nouveau decorations. In Bradley's designs, the sinuous lines of Art Nouveau combined beautifully with the straight lines of the Mission furniture. Unfortunately, they were never put into production.

Original Craftsman ("Mission") furniture designed by
Gustav Stickley and manufactured c. 1900. All oak.

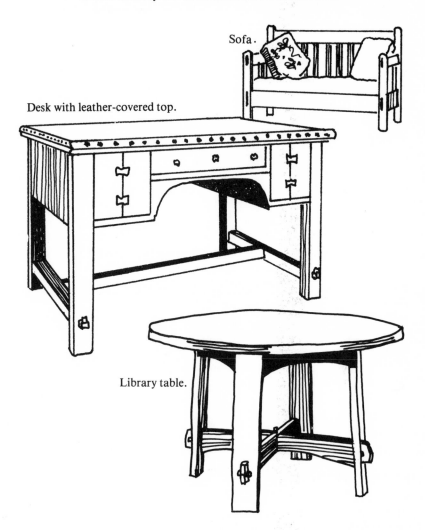

Sofa.

Desk with leather-covered top.

Library table.

Turn-of-the-century mail-order catalogs show Mission furniture as
one of three favored styles. The other two were "Golden Oak" and
"Colonial." Furniture in all three of these styles is quite common in
today's antique shops, so it is important to be able to recognize them.

Golden Oak is currently enjoying great popularity and, therefore,
increasing abnormally in value. In fact, many dealers believe that refinished and restored Golden Oak offers the most exceptional value in

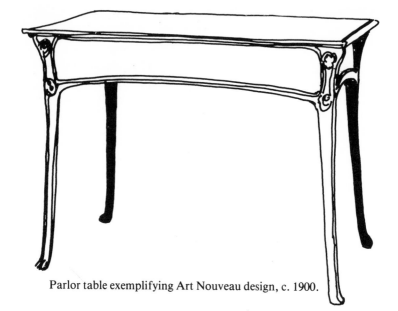

Parlor table exemplifying Art Nouveau design, c. 1900.

the antique business today. Although its style is distinctive, it doesn't resemble very much the styles that preceded it and, presumably, gave birth to it. Golden Oak is characterized by a moderate amount of machine carving, solid oak construction, and designs pressed into the wood in flat areas such as chair back, headboards, and mirrors. The style has also been called "Grand Rapids" because so much furniture of that type was manufactured in Grand Rapids, Michigan. But "Grand Rapids" is really a misnomer, for not all of that furniture was produced there, and the term is gradually dropping out of antiquarians' vocabulary.

One of the reasons that so much of this factory furniture was made of oak was that there were great oak forests in Wisconsin and Michigan, and, therefore, oak was a relatively inexpensive and available wood. Now, of course, oak ("the Abraham Lincoln of woods," Stickley called it—mahogany was to him "the George Washington of woods") has become comparatively scarce and expensive, in part accounting for the increased desirability of Golden Oak pieces.

The light color of Golden Oak was symptomatic of the changing tastes of the Late Victorian age. Stickley had replaced the dark, cluttered, ornate parlor of his early days with the living room, which was brighter, simpler, and had fewer pieces of furniture and bric-a-brac. Dark-toned mahogany and walnut were giving way to oak and other hardwoods in lighter shades, and this trend continued into the Twenties.

The third popular furniture style of the 1900s was "Colonial." This Colonial, as interpreted by vendors such as Montgomery Ward, Sears, Roebuck, and Spiegel, May, Stern Company, had no relationship that I can detect to any American Colonial style. It seemed to be, rather, an adaptation of the Late Empire style designed by John Hall. It had scroll feet, overhanging top drawers, and sleigh (then called "Napoleon") beds. Indeed, it is easy for shoppers to mistake furniture made in this style 75 years ago for scroll-footed pieces made 150 years ago.

Mail-order Colonial was made with thin walnut, oak, or mahogany veneers that usually did not hold up well as years passed. Chipped or peeling veneer is costly to replace and such a piece is not the bargain it may appear to be.

This bogus Colonial furniture was one facet of a growing interest in furniture design of colonial times. Early 20th century factories were busily turning out their versions of everything from 16th century English chairs to 18th century highboys, and those who were fortunate enough to have genuine colonial pieces stored away in family attics were dragging them downstairs and cleaning them up. Since that revival, at the turn of the century, interest in American colonial furniture has never really died. In the Midwest, however, there is so little genuine colonial furniture that one must be suspect of any piece reputed to be at least 200 years old. Dealers have been known to modify Victorian pieces in order to pass them off as colonial, so be sure of your dealer's reputation and ask for written verification if you buy such a piece.

One important difference between the original colonial furniture and the reproductions of the early 20th century is that the copies were generally made of inferior wood—and plywood at that, rather than solid wood. To conceal the poor quality of the wood underneath, reproductions were often painted with white or colored enamels.

By 1925, much of the flambuoyancy of previous styles had disappeared. There was still scroll-footed furniture, but the scrolls were restrained and delicate compared to those 20 years earlier. There was also furniture that showed French and English influences, but it, too, was tamed.

The furniture of the Twenties has not yet become fashionable. I say "not yet," because its day is surely coming. Thirty years ago, many people were condemning Victorian furniture as hopelessly tasteless. Now they are scrambling to collect it. If you or members of your

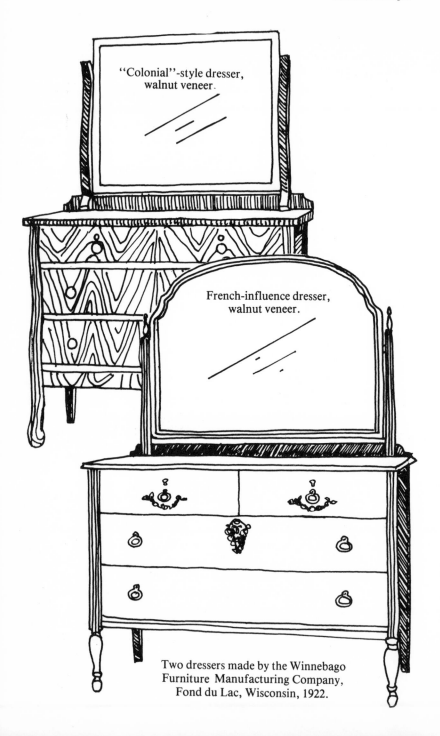

"Colonial"-style dresser, walnut veneer.

French-influence dresser, walnut veneer.

Two dressers made by the Winnebago Furniture Manufacturing Company, Fond du Lac, Wisconsin, 1922.

family own furniture that is now 50 years old, my advice is to hold on to it rather than give it away or sell it at a giveaway price. You yourself may never grow to love the styles of the Twenties, but at least you can be comforted by the thought that 25 years from now you will be able to sell that furniture for at least 20 times its original price.

Drawer pulls: (a) wooden knob, colonial times to present, side view; (b) brass knob, 1840-1850, side view; (c) pressed glass, 1830-1860, front view; (d), (e), (f) brass and wood, 1870-1885; (g) carved wood, usually leaves, 1870-1890; (h) brass, various designs, 1885-1900.

How Much to Pay and What to Look for in Living Room and Dining Room Furniture

Let's turn now to a description of some old furniture that is easily collectible in the Midwest. In most cases, I will give a range of prices for the items I describe. This approach is necessary because there are several factors that affect pricing: location of shop, condition of article, quality of workmanship, scarcity, type of wood, current fads.

In general, prices at auctions are lower than those in shops—probably about one-third lower. Away from the cities, prices are lower than in town—but then, you have to buy more gas, perhaps pay for motels and meals in order to save money by buying in the country. Remember that these are 1976 prices, and that you should add an average of 10-15 percent annually after that.

Mahogany and rosewood are at the top of the price scale. Next comes walnut, then oak. Pine, maple, butternut, and wild cherry are somewhat less. Least expensive are ash, birch, hickory, elm, and other native woods. If parts such as hardware or moldings have been replaced, the price should be lower than for intact pieces. If parts are missing, and you will have to replace them yourself, the asking price should be lower still.

If a wooden piece has been recently refinished by the dealer, the price will be about double what it would have cost had it not been refinished. In some shops, an article will be tagged with both an "as is" price and a refinished price, so you can see for yourself what the dealer figures refinishing is worth.

69

When furnishing a living room, my personal preference is to buy new upholstered sofas and chairs and combine them with antique pieces. The price of fabric and labor being what it is today, you probably will not save any money by buying old couches and chairs if you have to have someone else reupholster them. Of course, if you can do the reupholstering yourself, you will save money. Another factor to consider is that today's upholstered furniture is more comfortable than the Victorians'.

I do recognize, however, that for reasons of sentiment, self-accomplishment, and the desire for something unusual, some people may want to buy upholstered antique couches and chairs. As a rule of thumb, I consider that any old couch that needs complete reupholstering and refinishing should not cost more than $100—unless, of course, it is a candidate for a museum. Chairs in bad condition should be available for $25-$50. The cost of rehabilitation will probably be two or three times the purchase price.

The straight lines of American Empire sofas make them easier to reupholster than the later tufted and curved styles. In Victorian times, formal pieces were usually covered in horsehair, plush, damask, or velvet, but you are under no obligation to reupholster in an authentic fabric. In fact, unusual combinations may turn out to be even more interesting than traditional ones.

In good condition, Victorian couches cost $200-$300, although an elegant, velvet-upholstered medallion-back sofa that has been restored may have a price tag of $500-$600.

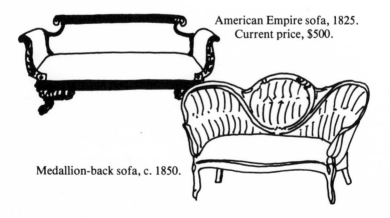

American Empire sofa, 1825.
Current price, $500.

Medallion-back sofa, c. 1850.

Small parlor table, oak, 1910.
Commonly offered for $25-$35.

Renaissance Revival oval parlor
table, walnut, made in Chicago, 1875.

Victorian chairs in good condition range from $75-$150. Recently I saw a refinished and reupholstered three-piece set in the Eastlake style (two small side chairs and a platform rocker) offered in a shop for $365. The set had been recovered in blue velvet, and was on the floor only a few days. "Fancy chairs" (the Hitchcock variety) are still available with their original stenciling. They are also in the $75-$150 category.

Small Victorian parlor tables (two to three feet across) are good buys. They were manufactured by the thousands—maybe millions—in such a variety of designs that you will probably never see two alike. They are relatively easy to refinish, although patience is required to remove the finish from intricate carvings. Small oak parlor tables 75 to 100 years old can be bought "as is" for as little as $25 in shops, somewhat less at auction, if you're lucky.

Parlor tables with marble tops are considerably more expensive. In Galena, Illinois, 100-year-old mahogany parlor tables with marble tops average $150. They would be more in a city. The asking price of a carved walnut, marble-topped parlor table in the Renaissance Revival style will be in the range of $150-$200. In cast iron instead of wood, a similar table will be $75-$100.

A popular and inexpensive antique item is the plant stand (also called a "fern stand"). Simple oak stands can be picked up at auction for $5 or $10 and for $12 to $25 in shops. Fancy ones are more, of course.

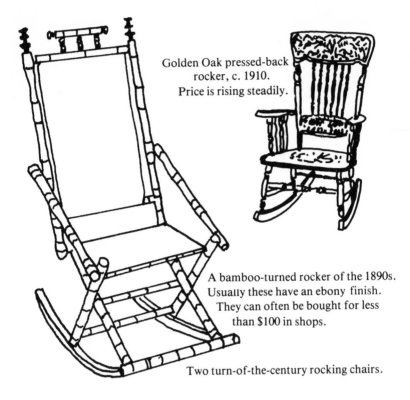

Golden Oak pressed-back
rocker, c. 1910.
Price is rising steadily.

A bamboo-turned rocker of the 1890s.
Usually these have an ebony finish.
They can often be bought for less
than $100 in shops.

Two turn-of-the-century rocking chairs.

You may want to consider buying a rocking chair for your living room—or porch, bedroom, den, or kitchen. Turn-of-the-century wooden rockers are plentiful. Pressed-back rockers that originally were sold through catalogs for $2 or $3 now cost at least $75 in fair condition. Many of these rockers originally came with fibreboard (then called "cobbler") seats which have broken up somewhere along the way. Usually these have been, or can be, replaced with cane seats. Others have shaped wooden seats to which you may want to add a pillow.

The pressed-back rocker is, of course, only one of innumerable kinds of rocking chairs that were made in the Midwest. Platform rockers, which were first made around 1870, can be found for $75 in poor condition. Reconditioned, they cost at least twice that.

Simple but charming wooden rockers without fancy designs (sometimes labeled "kitchen" rockers) can be purchased in good condition for as little as $35 in country shops. Larger, unusual rockers range from $75 to $150.

For reasons known only to Victorians, several types of folding rockers were manufactured in the last half of the 19th century. I have seen them in shops for $65 to $100, in good condition.

Windsor chairs can range in price from $5 to $1500. The $5 Windsor is the simple chair without arms that was commonly used in kitchens. A few months ago, a very old one, dated 1830, was on the floor of a Chicago area shop tagged $98. It was somewhat wobbly, but that is a malady that can usually be rather easily remedied. The $1500 Windsors are beautifully made survivors of 16th century England. You'll see them only at antique shows or in the classiest shops.

Slat-back chairs, with and without rockers, were made around the turn-of-the-century in Ontario in large numbers, and are still fairly common in the province. Used as porch (veranda) furniture, they have coarse turnings, long rockers, seats of splint (thin strips of wood, woven), and were originally painted green. They can still be purchased for $25 and up.

After languishing on old porches and in old attics since early in the century, a good deal of wicker furniture is being refurbished and resold. Wicker's longevity is not as great as that of wood because it is not very sturdy. You'll notice that many modestly priced wicker chairs and couches have holes in them, and they are real problems to repair. If you are interested in buying wicker, it's best to consider only pieces that are intact and need no more than spray-paint and recovered cushions to make them usable. (It is possible to remove old paint from wicker by stripping.)

As for prices, here are a few examples from recent notes: ordinary porch wicker armchair, repairable, $35; couch, good condition, $125; matching armchair, $60; wicker desk with walnut top and walnut chair, $125; matching round lamp table, $25; 1924 wicker sofa bed (yes, it opens up) and matching wicker rocker, $425; day bed (at auction), $75; wicker desk (at auction), $50.

Bamboo, which is usually thought of along with wicker, maintains a rather steady popularity, and occasionally you will come across a bamboo or simulated bamboo piece. In the past few months I have seen a bamboo easel (for displaying a painting) for $20 and a bamboo-turned folding rocker from the 1890s for $90. Small tables used to be a popular bamboo item, and they can be picked up for $20 or $30 today.

In 1866, in England, Morris & Co. designed an armchair with an adjustable back. It became immensely popular. Known as the "Morris chair," countless versions of it were manufactured during the succeeding 50 or 60 years. Unfortunately, the mechanisms of many eventually failed. However, if you find a Morris chair, it can usually be

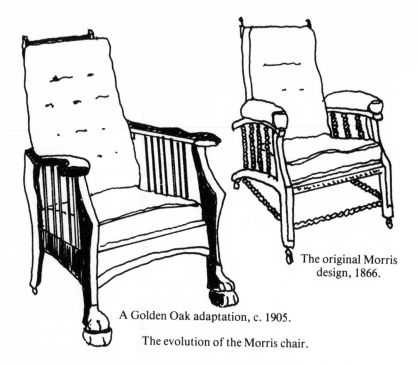

The original Morris
design, 1866.

A Golden Oak adaptation, c. 1905.

The evolution of the Morris chair.

restored to some degree of functioning. And even if it doesn't tilt back
(as is the case with ours), it is still a comfortable, not to say command-
ing, piece of furniture.

Dining rooms are much easier to furnish in antiques than living
rooms because you don't have to worry very much about upholstery.
Usually the most you have to do is replace slip seats on dining chairs,
and that can be done with little expertise.

In 1900 you could have bought an entire Golden Oak nine-piece
dining room suite (six chairs, table, sideboard, china cabinet) from a
mail-order catalog for $69.50. Similar sets at similar prices were avail-
able in the "Colonial" and Mission styles. Even at auction, that suite
will cost ten times $69.50 today.

Pressed-back dining chairs in the Golden Oak style are presently
among the hottest items on the American antique market today. At
the turn of the century, Montgomery Ward and others sold inexpensive versions of these chairs for $1.45 to $1.75 apiece, claiming that in
local stores similar chairs were selling for $2.50 to $3. Now, in poor
condition, in sets of four or six, they are $20 to $30 apiece; refinished,
as much as $80 apiece, and the price is up about a third from what it

Turn-of-the-century mail-order dining room suite, Golden Oak finish.
Original price for nine pieces, $69.50.

Mission-style dining room suite,
weathered oak finish,
1912, mail-order.

was last year. A single chair in poor condition can still be had for $8 or
$10. If buying things in sets is not essential to you, you can create an
interesting and unusual dining room by buying as many one-of-a-kind
chairs as you need. Pairs are often available, also.

The dining room table that goes with the pressed-back chairs is
Golden Oak, round, with a thick, carved pedestal. These tables range
between 42 and 48 inches wide. They may have several leaves and extend to 12 feet. Prices vary between $150 at auction and $350 refinished in a shop.

Golden Oak sideboards vary widely in price also. Plan to spend at
least $150 for a rather simple, small one; up to $550 for an elaborately
carved piece with leaded glass panels.

China cabinets with curved glass sides start at about $150 also, but
are usually in the $250 category.

Another dining room piece is the vertical buffet. It usually has a
narrow china cabinet on one side and a mirror, drawers, and a cabinet
with drawers on the right. This piece is not as commonly seen as its
sister, a secretary-bookcase, sometimes called a "side-by-side," which
generally has a bookcase on one side and a drop-front desk, drawers
and mirror on the other. The buffets and side-by-sides were all-pur-
pose pieces that now cost from $165 to $500.

Combination desk and bookcase of the Golden Oak period. Often called, in the Midwest, a "side-by-side."

Currently of great popularity, the Golden Oak pedestal dining table.

Two Golden Oak dining room chairs from the Montgomery Ward catalog of 1912.

Seat is ash. Original price was $1.75.   Seat is cane. Original price, $1.45.

There are also sideboards both older and younger than the Golden Oak variety that are available at lower prices, but some elaborate examples were expensive when they were new and still are today. And you'll see some really massive sideboards that are inexpensive. If you wonder why, consider the size—there are not many potential buyers.

In areas where there are a lot of big, 50-year-old homes you'll probably see a lot of big, 50-year-old dining room furniture. Typically, it is styled after Jacobean furniture of Renaissance England. In the trade it was called "Grand Rapids Tudor," because quantities of it came out of Grand Rapids factories. You should be able to purchase it at reasonable prices. The problem, of course, is that you have to have a large room to house it. If you have that, and patience as well, you can sit back and wait while the furniture appreciates in value over the next 25 years.

Hall furniture is another facet of the antique business that is currently experiencing a boom. You probably remember that your grandmother or great-grandmother had a wooden monstrosity in the entrance hall of her house or apartment with a looking-glass and repositories for your umbrella, hat, coat, and boots. Useful as it was, that monstrosity became distinctly unfashionable during the Twenties, and not until the past couple of years has anybody really cared what happened to it. Now, even if you find a beat-up old hallstand that you think no one else would want to bother to restore, you can hardly pry it out of the dealer's hands. *He* wants to restore it and make a bigger profit.

Well, if you have the space for it, I advise you to buy a hallstand—any kind of hallstand—and do whatever you have to do to fix it up. Refinished, a simple one costs $200 and up. Weird specimens, especially those with seats (strictly speaking, they're hall*seats*), sell for $300-$400. But take heart: Hallstands in deplorable condition can be found for $50-$75. Oak hall mirrors with hooks for coats and hats run about $100. Hatstands in wood can be had for $25; in brass, for $65 at auction; and for $75-$100 in a shop, if you can find them.

If your living room or family room has a fireplace, you may want to consider installing an old mantel. These can be found in the junk shop sections of antique shops—in the back, upstairs, or in the alley. I have never seen an old, fully restored mantel for sale in a shop, but I have seen some in homes, and they can be lovely. In the Midwest, you can find some really strange-looking ones, buried beneath heavy layers of varnish or paint, at prices that start at $65.

Suppose you have a room in your home that you'd like to furnish as an office. For desks, you can run the gamut of a plain oak used desk

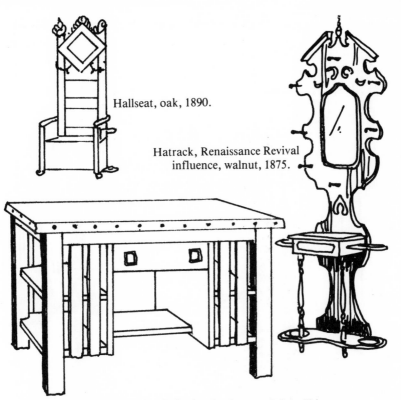

Hallseat, oak, 1890.

Hatrack, Renaissance Revival
influence, walnut, 1875.

Mission-style desk, mail order, imitation leather, made in a Chicago
factory and sold by mail order. Original price, $10.90.

for $25 to a Wooten patent desk for $3000-$4000. In between are
Mission-style desks for $50 to $125 and rolltop desks (in my opinion, a
vastly overrated and impractical item—the rolltop is usually *very* stiff)
for $250-$300. Stacking bookcases made of oak by the Globe Company in Cincinnati in 1900 are selling for $100 to $150, depending
upon condition and size. Mission oak stacking bookcases (same
period) run about the same. Globe Company oak filing cabinets with
four or five drawers are also $100 to $150 in fair to good condition,
somewhat less in poor condition.

Actually, desks are ubiquitous items. They were, and still are, used
in many different rooms. Small slant-front desks were made for parlors, offices, schoolrooms; fall-fronts (the desk shelf folds up verti-
cally to look like a drawer) for wherever a desk was useful. An old
slant-front desk crafted by a Midwestern cabinetmaker in pine and
oak was recently for sale on the floor of a shop near Chicago. An
unusual country piece, it was priced at $295.

How Much to Pay and What to Look for in Bedroom and Kitchen Furniture

Bedrooms can be easily and, if you choose, inexpensively furnished with Victorian antiques. You can spend a lot of money for a bed or you can spend almost none at all. An American Empire high four-poster will cost you $1000-$1500. Double-size brass beds, restored, are going for $400-$500. (These can accommodate an outsize mattress if extensions are added to the frame.) And you might be able to find a painted brass bed, twin size, that has to be stripped and refinished, for $150. Twenty-five years ago, these beds were being carted away as junk. But the brass-bed craze developed, and prices zoomed upward, where they have remained ever since.

Seventy years ago, the top of the mail-order line of brass beds sold for $20; less expensive ones ran from $10 to $20. Better quality beds cost two or three times that. An alternative, then as now, was an iron bed with brass knobs and other trim. Depending upon the amount of brass trim, which runs the price up, these beds can be bought today for as little as $90 at auction, refinished. Today the iron portions are usually painted with black enamel, the brass with clear varnish; and the result is very attractive.

Away from cities, all-iron or iron-steel beds can be picked up for $30-$75. Most iron beds originally had a white enamel finish, and they were frequently sold as part of a bedroom suite in which the two other pieces—a dresser and a commode—were Golden Oak. The dresser had an attached mirror and several drawers. The commode usually had one drawer and two doors and, at the top, a towel rack.

Golden Oak bedroom suites with wooden beds were also very popular and are fairly common in antique shops. When they are of good

Mail-order brass bed. Original price, $10.65.

Carved wooden bed, Golden Oak, from an Indiana factory.

quality and are in good condition, they go for about $600. A single heavy, good-quality Golden Oak dresser might be tagged $325; a commode, $145; and a bed, $185.

Miscellaneous wooden beds 50 to 100 years old can be bought for as little as $50-$75. Many need no more than cleaning up to be presentable. More choice specimens will be $100-$300.

Interesting beds at reasonable prices seem to be more readily available in Ontario than in the Midwest. Under-eaves beds, dating from before 1860, can still be found for $50, for they are not very popular. They were made to be used in rooms with sloping ceilings, and are simple, even crude. Many were built by handymen. Another good buy in Ontario beds is the dark-finished Victorian spool bed with paneled ends. They are available for $50 to $200. Because their head- and footboards are the same height, they can be placed side-by-side and used as the headboards of twin beds. But you may decide to have a bed with no head- and footboard at all. All you really need is a metal frame on which to rest your mattress and springs. In that case, you can buy or make a bedspread that will complement the antique furnishings in the room, and decorate the wall above the bed with paintings, objects, photographs, a mirror.

Turn-of-the-century mail-order bedroom suite. Iron bed, oak dresser and commode with towel rack. Original price, $18.95 complete.

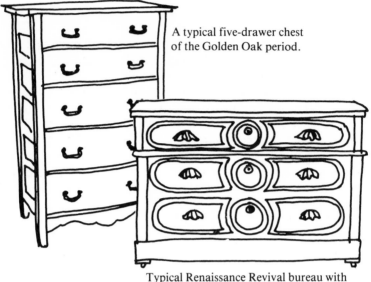

A typical five-drawer chest
of the Golden Oak period.

Typical Renaissance Revival bureau with
carved-leaf drawer pulls. May have marble top.

Eastlake dressers in walnut with teardrop pulls, which date them in
the 1870s or 1880s, can be found for $250 to $350, depending upon
locale and condition. But be forewarned that the Eastlake style, so
much maligned 20 years ago, has now reached a level of respectability
that has pushed up the price. An Eastlake bed with burled walnut
panels might be priced at $550; in plain walnut, $350. Walnut dressers
with carved-leaf pulls from the second half of the 19th century sell for
between $175 and $275.

If all you need is a functional, inexpensive dresser, you have a wide
choice. They are plentiful, and you can pick one up in usable condition for $75-$100—as low as $50 if you're willing to spend some time
and money fixing it up. But beware of dressers with thin, peeling
veneer—they are practically impossible to restore without spending
more money than the piece is worth. Bogus Colonial from the turn-of-
the-century and inexpensive bedroom suites from the 1920s are likely
to be in this category.

"Colonial"-style dresser. May be oak, or mahogany or walnut veneer. Cheap versions usually in poor condition these days.

Renaissance Revival dresser, walnut, c. 1885.
May have either teardrop or carved-leaf drawer pulls.

Water bench, pine, early 19th c. Wash basins and pitchers
were stored in cabinet, set on lower shelf for use.

Washstands and bedside tables are much harder to find than
dressers, chests, and beds. Washstands, popular before the advent of
indoor plumbing, usually consisted of a small table with a lower shelf
on which sat a washbowl and pitcher. Usually there were rods on
either side of the top on which towels were hung. Stripped or refinished, they sell for about $100 or $125 in shops. The usual wood is
maple; some are wild cherry. Legs with spool turnings are not
uncommon, but beware of reproductions.

Small cupboards that can be used as bedside tables are available;
however, I have searched for three years, without success, for a
matched pair to put on either side of a double bed. If I ever find a
pair, I expect they will be $75-$100 apiece, in good condition.

Small dressers, some with only one drawer, were also used for Victorian toilettes. Often a separate mirror sat on top. There were also
shaving stands with a number of conveniences: towel racks, a mirror,
a couple of shelves, perhaps a couple of drawers. Toilet accessories
like the last few mentioned are more decorative than functional these
days, since it's unlikely that they will actually be used for washing and

shaving unless there's a line for the bathroom. But, of course, you can set such items on them as lamps, books or radios. Another item that has become passe with changing architecture is the armoire. Not until after the turn of the century were closets built in houses, so Victorians used large cupboards, called armoires or wardrobes, to hold their clothes. Armoires are not fast-selling pieces these days, so you may be able to talk a dealer down on the asking price, whatever it is.

Blanket chests were useful items in pioneer homes. Some of the most interesting chests, those of Scandinavian design, usually had curved tops and handpainted decorations on the outside. In Ontario before 1850, the settlers made wooden dome-top chests that were covered with deerhide or painted; some were decorated with brass studs. Six-board blanket chests were usually made of pine, rarely of hardwood. Depending upon age, condition, and desirability, blanket chests will range from $50 to several hundred. But they are more a colonial than a Victorian item, and early blanket chests are not very often seen in Midwest antique shops.

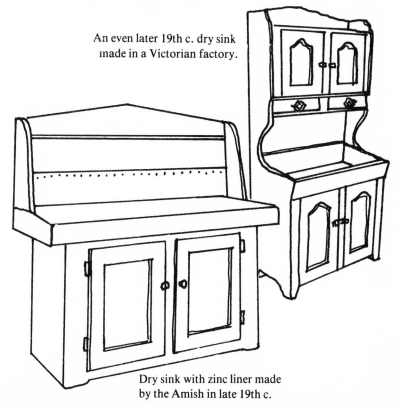

An even later 19th c. dry sink made in a Victorian factory.

Dry sink with zinc liner made by the Amish in late 19th c.

There are, however, a number of old trunks around that you can make into inexpensive, attractive blanket and storage chests, for after mid-19th century, factories made wooden chests covered with canvas, and these can be picked up for very little cash. At a recent garage sale for sophisticates, I saw a lovely old wooden trunk with a curved lid that had been stripped to bare wood and then given a soft, clear finish. Quite large and handsome, it was snapped up by an early-bird shopper for $60. Smaller trunks that need restoration are commonly available for about $25. When considering buying a particular trunk, remember that replacement hardware and handles can be purchased (see Chapter 9). Original decoration and identification becomes more interesting and valuable with time, so think carefully before you destroy any.

If you have room for it, a rocking chair is nice in the bedroom (see Chapter 7 for descriptions). A rocker is particularly appropriate, not to mention useful, in a nursery, for its original purpose was to help harassed babysitters soothe fretful infants. The rocker has experienced a resurgence in popularity in modern times, particularly since the publicity that accompanied President Kennedy's use of a rocking chair as therapy for an ailing back. But, if you don't have space for a rocker, a Victorian side chair (see Chapter 7) will do nicely to complete the antique furnishings for your bedroom.

Now for utility furniture in the kitchen. Combining the gleaming chrome, porcelain, and stainless steel of today's kitchens with the patina of well-used antique pieces can be particularly interesting. But if you have a small, modern kitchen jammed with appliances, it may be impossible.

Consider what the kitchen was to early Midwesterners. In pioneer houses, it was the most important room. At first, it was the only room that was heated—by the cooking stove. The bedrooms were small; sometimes they were just a loft or a had a plank bed nailed to a wall. Often a homesteader built a parlor onto his house, and used it only for guests on Sunday. For the most part, family life revolved around the kitchen. Later, as houses became more elaborate, there were more rooms, and kitchens lost some of their functions to dining rooms, parlors, and porches. Still, in all except city flats, kitchens were large and held a lot of furniture. Cupboards were freestanding, not the built-ins we know today. There were large tables, some with bins for flour and dough. Other workspace was provided by cabinets, which had cupboards and shelves for storage and an overhanging counter where a food grinder was mounted.

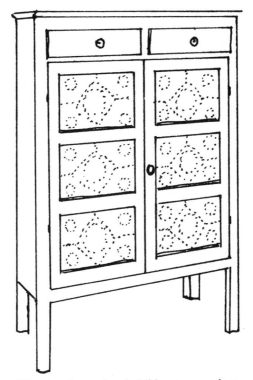

The pie safe, a uniquely Midwestern product.
This one has pierced-tin panels and was made by hand about 1850.

There were also kitchen "safes"—cupboards that had no counter space, but were used to store dishes and kitchen utensils. Early kitchen safes had solid wooden doors or panels of pierced tin. Fanciful designs in the tin made these cupboards (usually called "pie safes" in the Midwest) interesting pieces. They were originally built to keep flies away from the food stored in them, while still letting air circulate around them. At a later date, glass doors were put in kitchen cupboards that were used to store dishes.

Any of these large kitchen cabinets and cupboards will cost you at least $150. It is hard to find a pie safe in good condition for less than $250, but sometimes a bargain can be had if the piece is covered with several layers of paint.

A few years ago, dry sinks were a fad of antiquarians. Now, I doubt you'll find one around that hasn't already been refinished and resold. A dry sink is a wooden cupboard that has, usually, a sink—sometimes lined with zinc or copper or other metal—a drainboard, and, at the

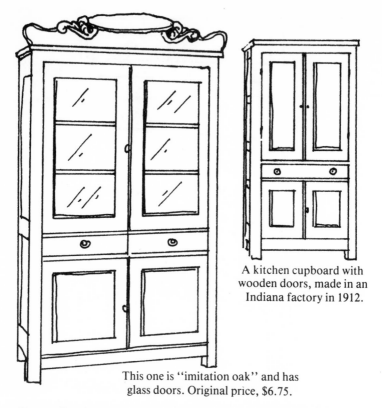

A kitchen cupboard with
wooden doors, made in an
Indiana factory in 1912.

This one is "imitation oak" and has
glass doors. Original price, $6.75.

Two mail-order kitchen cupboards from the first decade of this century.

back, a splashboard. Sometimes there is a cupboard above, as well. Typically, dry sinks were made of pine or butternut. In the Midwest, they were used for various kitchen chores, including washing dishes, until the turn of the century. In the East, they dropped out of popular use earlier, and there they are regarded, or at least passed off, as colonial pieces. Because they have for years been so much sought after, dry sinks are now priced between $200 and $300, depending upon size, and a bargain is hard to come by.

A similar, but less commonly seen kitchen piece is the water bench, which was used for essentially the same purposes as the dry sink. It has cupboards in the lower half for storing pans, pails, and basins; a counter; and, usually, a shelf at the top with perhaps a few shallow drawers. Another popular storage piece from the Midwest is the jelly cupboard. It has a cupboard below with two doors and there are two drawers above the cupboard. Depending upon size and condition, these will cost $150-$250.

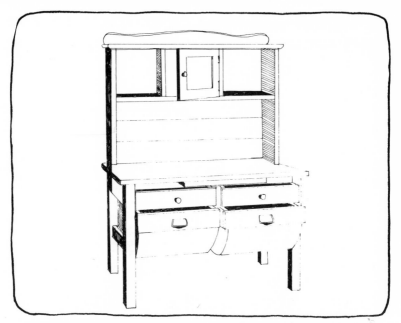

The "latest sanitary design" in mail-order kitchen cabinets, made about 1900 in a central Indiana factory. You could have bought it for $1.25 down, and 75 cents monthly. Total price, $7.95.

Turn-of-the-century oak iceboxes are also very popular with modern collectors. They stand four to five feet high and usually have two or three doors that open in the front. Fancy ones may have a mirror also. Small, plain ice boxes in need of refinishing can still be picked up for about $100. Refinished, the bottom price these days is $150. Again, depending upon size, condition, and degree of elaborateness, the ice boxes may sell for $350—occasionally even more. At an auction I watched as an elegantly carved, claw-footed model with an oval mirror in the top door sold for $320. In a shop, it would easily be worth $500.

In 1900 John M. Smyth Company's Mammoth Mail-Order House in Chicago sold Puritan refrigerators. These were made of ash and had a lift-top for the ice chamber and one or two doors in the front. They sold for $7 to $17.50 and they carried this comforting guarantee, as stated in the catalog:

"Puritan cleanable refrigerators are built with eight walls. This is one of the places where it is easy to deceive a buyer. All you can see is the wood outside and the zinc inside. What there is between you don't know, but our guarantee makes you safe."

The late Victorian icebox.
In oak, heavily carved, with mirror.

In ash, from the John M. Smyth
catalog of 1900.

I have not personally seen a Puritan brand icebox, but I have seen similar ones in shops, priced at $150. And a handsome, large, oak specimen with brass hardware, the "New Perfection," made by the Belding Manufacturing Company, Belding, Michigan, was recently tagged $335.

A note of caution: Don't buy an old icebox without checking the inside. I have seen many a one that looked dandy from the outside, but was pretty awful on the inside. If you want to use the icebox for storage, the zinc liner and galvanized iron shelves can be cleaned and then painted or covered with cloth.

Butcher blocks, all the rage a few years ago, have had their heyday. Most of the genuinely old ones were bought up by collectors for use as tables of various types, with or without their legs. There was a time when you could buy one for $25 or $50, treat the wood, and have a nice old piece. Now, even a small one in disrepair (with chunks of wood missing, legs broken) costs at least $150.

Kitchen tables are plentiful. One very popular style, the oval drop-leaf with turned legs, can easily be picked up for $40 or $50 if you refinish it yourself, particularly if it is made of one of the less desirable woods. I saw one in black walnut, evidently the work of a country craftsman of 75-100 years ago, go for $70 at auction. Black walnut of course, is a *desirable* wood.

A table that takes up a good deal more space, but which is very charming, is the five-legged style. (The fifth leg is in the center of the table.) In oak, they can be bought for $100 at auction, in good condition—about $150 in shops. When refinished, the old five-legged tables look beautiful, and you may decide to use it in your dining room instead. In fact, any of these kitchen pieces can be charmingly used in other rooms. I am putting furniture in categories by rooms only for the sake of organization.

Kitchen chairs were something even the poorest, most isolated homes had to have. They were well used, and many, of course, have been consigned to the junk heap through the years. But there are still lots of old Windsors around, although they are often struggling to breathe through layers of paint and dirt. If you care enough to reclaim them, you can buy them for as little as $5 apiece. Bentwood chairs of doubtful age can be bought for $10 to $15 each. Pressed-back chairs are nice for the kitchen, too, although at today's prices, you may want to save them for the dining room (see Chapter 7).

Your family and friends will love a rocker in the kitchen. Many old farmhouses had them, and if you spend $25 or $30 to buy one and restore it, it'll give you much pleasure—maybe even a memory of a great-grandmother shucking corn, shelling peas—and rocking near the warmth of an old stove.

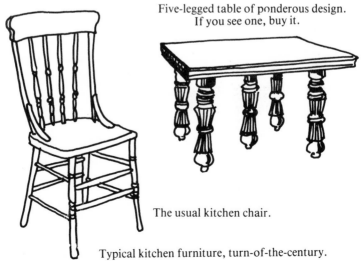

Five-legged table of ponderous design.
If you see one, buy it.

The usual kitchen chair.

Typical kitchen furniture, turn-of-the-century.

How to Act in Antique Shops and at Auctions and Other Sales

A number of people have said to me, "Oh, I'd love to have some antiques, but I don't know anything about them, and I'm afraid to go in an antique shop—I'd probably get cheated."

Well, if you've gotten this far in this book, you already know more than most shoppers do about antiques in the Midwest. And to further fortify you, I'm going to take this chapter to discuss some of the ways and places in which to shop.

The most obvious place is the antique shop. You'll find that the personalities of shops vary with each owner. The better the shop (that is, the higher the prices and the quality of the merchandise), the more knowledgeable and sophisticated the person who runs it. Those who are members of local or national antique dealers' associations can generally be depended upon to give you good information about the furniture in the shop and to sell it for an honest profit. Not that there aren't honest and knowledgeable dealers who aren't members of associations—there certainly are. It's just that your chances of getting taken are less in established shops.

When you buy a quality antique from such a dealer, you should get a written statement regarding the authenticity of your purchase. If you have the money, that's the safest and sanest way to buy antiques. Just go to a dealer whose store is in the best part of town, find something you like and buy it with confidence, knowing that if you decide to re-sell the item at a future date, it will always be worth at least what you paid for it—unless economic disaster overtakes us all, in which case even your gold bullion may be a bit shaky.

That's the ideal. Fortunately or unfortunately, depending upon your viewpoint, most of us cannot operate that way. We have to scrounge around, take some chances, actually gamble a bit with our time and our money to acquire some old furniture that may or may not someday earn the classification of "antique." It's sort of a game, and you're going to learn how to play.

To begin with, you should know how antique dealers acquire the things they sell. Most antique retailers buy their merchandise from wholesalers, just as in any other business. Run-of-the-mill antiques, the kind you and I would buy, are delivered by wholesalers in lots as large as 40-foot vans, to antique shops. Some dealers sell on both a wholesale and retail basis, and other retailers buy small lots or individual items from them. Sometimes orders are placed over the telephone, sometimes by mail. Other times retailers go to the wholesale houses with their own trucks and pick up antiques they will resell. If you read the weekly newspaper of the antique trade, *The Antique Trader Weekly,* you'll see ads placed by large wholesale outfits in different parts of the country. *The Trader* is available at many public libraries, or you can order a subscription or a copy of a single issue from P.O. Box 1050, Dubuque, Iowa 52001.

Of course, it would be nice to be able to shop at the wholesale barns as an individual, but as far as I know it's not possible unless you know someone there personally. Most "wholesale only" dealers are very careful about maintaining that category. If you visit a dealer who sells both wholesale and retail, be aware that there will be one price for you, a lower one for a dealer.

Retailers also get their merchandise from "pickers," people who actually go out into the countryside, buying old furniture from farms and small towns and auctions. These pickers have shop owners who are their regular customers. Sometimes the shop owners look over what the pickers have in the truck and buy what they want. Other times, shop owners will have requests from particular customers that they pass along to the pickers, who then try to find those items in their travels.

Knowing about wholesalers and pickers may destroy some of the fantasy we start out with—that of the friendly antique dealer visiting with his friends and neighbors, who give him their family heirlooms to offer to us—but the fact is that the dealer wouldn't have time to keep his shop open if he spent all those hours visiting around.

There really are some people who offer their family heirlooms to antique dealers, but not enough to supply the whole antique trade. Most retailers do a good deal of trading, with customers as well as other dealers. If there's a particular item that a dealer feels one of her customers would want, she'll buy from or trade with whoever has it. And there really are some dealers who are fortunate enough to have someone else keep the shop open and who do most of their own shopping, buying from individuals and at auctions.

Also—as I have indicated—there are quite a few retail shops that buy reproductions and sell them along with their antique stock. Usually, if you ask, the dealer will tell you frankly if an item you are interested in is a reproduction or not. But remember—you have to *ask*. You can't count on a dealer to volunteer the information.

An old piece of furniture smells old, it is worn in spots, it may show evidence of several layers of paint or varnish at the joints. There are other ways to tell whether a piece is genuinely old, but they're for the experts. The best you can do as a novice is to trust your senses—smell the piece, run your hand over it, look at it carefully. Nothing can exist for 50 or 100 years and not show a few bruises. If it seems too slick, don't trust it. And, don't forget—*ask*. Ask what the dealer knows about the piece—its age, the kind of wood, where it came from, what defects it has, how to repair or refinish it. You may not believe or follow all the advice you get, but I guarantee you, you'll learn *something*.

I distrust any smart-looking shop that sells cheese, candy, or candles. A lot of such places also sell reproductions, and the antiques they do have are refinished and expensive. You'll find this type of shop in areas where there are many antique dealers—they are usually johnny-come-latelies who are anxious to cash in on the tourist boom. In those same touristy areas, however, you can find some shops that do offer genuinely old furniture at moderate prices. Again, trust yourself to tell the difference.

You'll often find that certain sections in metropolitan areas abound in antique shops. They are usually the old parts of town, where the houses are finally giving up their yesteryear treasures—the occupants are passing on, or the buildings are being torn down to make way for chrome and cement high-rises or urban renewal projects. Some of these in-town shops are mainly repositories for junk, but that's okay. Some of my own best-loved possessions came from such junk shops. They are often run by young people—as opposed to country antique shops, which are run mostly by older people—and that's okay, too—just be a little cautious everywhere.

You'll notice that some dealers sell only furniture that's in good condition or refinished. That's because the profit margin is higher. There's nothing wrong with patronizing that kind of shop if you don't want to be bothered with refinishing, but be prepared for somewhat higher prices.

My own favorite kind of antique shop is one that's out in the country and is operated by people who have been in business there for years. The shop is packed to the ceiling with stuff, most of which is sold "as is." It's dirty and dusty there, and you have to move things to get a good look at what might be buried treasure. If the price on the tag isn't so low you'd feel guilty bargaining, offer the dealer something less, pointing out the defects of the piece, and being careful not to act too enthusiastic. The bargain struck, you'll carry away your purchase yourself, both sides happy with the transaction. It's great fun.

Auctions can be fun, too, as people infected with auction fever will be delighted to tell you. Here's what to expect. There are some auction houses that have regularly scheduled sales—maybe once a month, or twice a month, in their own warehouses. The auctioneers take whole estates, or parts of estates, usually on consignment, and resell them to dealers or collectors. (That's what the individual customer is called in the trade—a collector.) That's one kind of auction.

Other auction services hold sales on a fairly regular basis, rotating among several locations, such as particular motels that have large rooms suitable for auction activities. These sales are advertised in metropolitan papers (under classified sections called "Auctions" or "Antiques"), in suburban newspapers, and in antique trade publications. My favorite, *The Antique Trader Weekly*, runs listings of antique sales for different areas of the country. *The Trader's* three categories are "Auction," "Show," and "Flea Market." Auction services also run display ads in *The Trader*, often giving details about the items that will be offered at specific sales.

When you go to an auction, you will be asked to register, and then you will be given a card with a number on it. Occasionally, if it is an important sale, there is an admittance fee, which will be applied to any purchase you make. Usually, there is no charge. It's best to arrive a half hour to an hour before the sale begins so that you can look over the merchandise. At really big auction sales, you will need more time. Doors will open before—sometimes hours or days before—the bidding begins to give prospective buyers time for inspection.

If you see something you are interested in bidding on, look it over carefully and decide how much you are willing to spend for it. Then, when the bidding gets going, try to stick to your limit—otherwise, you might get carried away. If the sale is well run, the bidding moves fast. At first, the auctioneer will offer some small items—glassware, china, lamps, collectibles such as harpoons, flags, military equipment. Unless most of the audience is interested in that kind of thing, the smart auctioneer will move on to larger items of furniture, perhaps returning to the miscellany later.

If the auctioneer who "cries" the sale (the trade term) is called "Colonel," he is a graduate of a school of auctioneering. Students live at these schools for a two-week term, attending classes that teach them the auctioneer's chant, facts about different kinds of selling (farm, auto, real estate, livestock, antiques, tobacco), how to make sales talks and tell jokes, how to manage auction sales.

The auctioneer usually has several floor assistants. They hold up the item being offered, or at least bring it out in front of the audience where it can be seen. They watch the audience for bidders, calling out "Yes!", whenever a person bids the price being asked at that moment by the auctioneer. If you wind up as the successful bidder on a small item, an assistant will bring it over to your seat. Sometimes two or more of the same type of item will be offered at one time, and the auctioneer usually explains that the purchaser can choose one, or take them all at multiples of the bid price. Be sure you understand how many items you are bidding on before you do it. Otherwise, you may find you have bought six regimental flags when you thought you were buying only one!

Generally, the auctioneer will start out at a price higher than he expects anyone to bid, then quickly drops down until he gets the bidding started. To make a bid, a person usually needs only to raise a hand. If you want to look like a pro, hold up your card with your number on it. It's hardly ever necessary to call out a bid. If you're sitting in the front row and the auctioneer knows you're bidding, a motion with your hand is sufficient. Don't take your knitting—you may confuse the poor auctioneer. If you're sitting farther back, try not to scratch your head or pull your ear while the bidding is going on—you might wind up with a mounted elk head you don't want.

Bidding moves fast, so listen closely to the auctioneer's opening speech about an item you're interested in, then follow the action carefully. Bidding on an item is usually all over in a couple of minutes. The auctioneer will announce beforehand whether delivery service is available or whether you have to take with you whatever you buy. Some auction services do not accept personal checks—only traveler's checks, certified checks, or cash. To avoid embarrassment, find out about these arrangements before you start bidding.

The general rule of auctions is that you buy what you see. Nothing is guaranteed unless specifically so stated by the auctioneer. And unless an article is definitely misrepresented by the auctioneer, you can't change your mind and decide not to take something after you have bought it. And there are no exchange privileges.

Once you attend an auction, you will probably receive fliers in the mail advertising subsequent sales held by the same service. This is especially helpful if you are interested in a particular type of item—an oak hallseat, for example—because the fliers usually list items that will be offered on a specified date. One of the things you have to accept about auctions is that they go on for hours, and the item you want may be the last one on the agenda—or it may even be held over until the next sale if the hour gets too late.

Auctions are not the only places to pick up old furniture at less than shop prices. There are also flea markets and estate, garage, and basement sales. These sales may be advertised in city or local newspapers, as well as by street posters and fliers.

Flea markets are becoming much more popular and numerous than they used to be. At flea markets, many different dealers offer their merchandise at small stands or selling spaces. They may be held inside or outside; they may be held regularly, or only on special occasions. I do not think that, as a rule, flea markets offer as much to furniture buyers as to collectors of smaller antiques. But that situation may be changing too, because more and more frequently antique sales and flea markets are being combined into the same events. If you think you would like shopping in this manner, visit a few flea markets in your area to find out if they're what you're looking for.

Estate sales occur after someone dies, leaving possessions that must be disposed of outside the family, or when someone who has maintained a large household moves—to a new job elsewhere, smaller quarters, or a warmer climate. A sale service takes over, prices everything to be sold, advertises the sale, and conducts it. The really neat estate sales take place in old mansions that have housed the furniture for generations, and you should watch your newspapers for notices of sales like these. And go early. You may find something right away that you want and can afford. Then you pay the asking price. If there's something you like but can't afford, inquire about putting in a bid and returning on the last day of the sale. You may be able to buy it then at the price you bid.

Occasionally, household sales yield some bargains in antiques. You should keep in mind, though, that you might not be dealing with innocents. An increasing number of private collectors are becoming semiprofessional antique dealers. They buy more antiques than they can personally use, refinish and restore them, and then sell off the excess at garage sales. Prices are likely to be somewhat more than at auction, somewhat less than in shops, and the chances of finding just what you want are less than usual. Still, if you're an antiquarian, they're worth a look.

Antique shows offer some special benefits. The antiques displayed there are likely to be of top quality and they command top prices. At shows, you will see the best on the market, and the experience can be quite educational as well as entertaining. Exhibitors will be standing around with hours of idle time on their hands, often eager to answer your questions. A few will look down their noses at you, which is annoying, but don't let it put you off entirely. After all, you paid your admission and you're entitled, right?

How to Restore Old Furniture

As the popularity of antiques grows, so does the number of refinishing products and processes. Since everyone seems to develop his or her own favorite methods, my purpose in this chapter is merely to give some general advice and mention some specific possibilities and problems.

The matter of repairing and refinishing is, first of all, something that should be considered when you are deciding whether or not to buy a piece of furniture. Keep in mind that it will not be an antique if you have to replace more than 10 percent of it. And, unless it has sentimental value, you do not want to spend more money restoring it than you could sell it for in restored condition.

Be particularly careful about buying old beds. Many of them will not accommodate today's standard-size mattresses and springs. Be sure to ask the dealer how the bed can be adapted without having to have mattress and springs specially made—that can be very expensive. One of the easiest conversion techniques is to remove the old siderails and slats (or ropes, if it is a *very* old bed), fit a Hollywood bed inside, and attach the head- and footboards to it with angle irons. A full-width bedspread or dust ruffle will hide the extra legs. *Do not* throw away the old slats and siderails. Keep these pieces, so that if any time in the future someone wants to put the original pieces back together again, they will be available.

In general, if a chair or table is wobbly, the joints can be reglued and the piece made sturdy once more. If there is something seriously wrong with a leg or a rung (it is broken or missing), I would not advise buying the piece unless you have more than an amateur standing as a woodworker, or you are willing to pay to have the repairs done.

Warping of a table top or a split in it is considered an authenticator of age. Unless it impairs function, it should not be judged a value-lowering defect, and it should not be repaired. Severe warping of a cabinet door may mean, however, that the door will never close correctly. If dove-tailing (the wedge-shaped pieces that hold drawers together) is broken, don't buy the piece.

Don't buy wicker furniture that has holes in it—or any furniture with holes that have to be repaired unless you have a pretty good idea how they *can* be repaired.

Be wary of furniture with several coats of paint. The paint may hide serious problems, different kinds of wood or inferior wood, or repairs. Some people would never buy a painted piece, but I think this attitude is foolish. Underneath the layers of gook may be beautiful oak or walnut just waiting to be freed from its stifling cover. Often, the dealer will have removed paint from just a small area, so that prospective buyers can see what the wood looks like. If not, you can ask the dealer to let you chip away a small amount of paint so you can see what is underneath.

Inexpensive furniture on which veneer is chipped or peeling is a nearly hopeless situation. It might still be functional, but it will probably never be beautiful. If the piece is of better quality, it may be worthwhile to have the veneer replaced, and you should consult about that possibility with your dealer, and, if possible, with a cabinetmaker before buying.

Those are about the only situations in which I would not buy an old piece of furniture even if I liked it. Practically everything else can be fixed.

Basic tools for simple furniture repairs include pliers, screwdrivers, hammers, scrapers, and a file. You will need clamps to hold parts together until all fresh glue has dried, but in an emergency, you can wrap heavy string around the glued parts and tighten it up with a pencil, tourniquet fashion.

Let us suppose you have bought a piece of furniture that you knew needed some repairs. Now that you have it at home, you are anxious to examine it again. You should have looked at the piece in a strong light before you bought it. Take a second look now.

Are any parts missing, such as pieces of molding, finials (carved decorative ends), hardware, hinges, nails, or screws? These are the things you will have to make, buy, or have made, and that sometimes takes weeks. You may need to have some work done by a professional cabinetmaker, or you may at least want to get the advice of a professional. Sometimes the dealer from whom you bought the piece can repair it for you, or will recommend someone who can do it. If not, look in your classified telephone directory under categories such as

"Furniture Repairing," "Upholsterers," "Antiques—Repairing and Restoring."

If the piece is small enough to transport easily, take it with you to a couple of these places for estimates and advice. If it is too large to move, see if you can remove a part similar to or exactly like the one that has to be replaced and take it to the woodworker. Be very careful when prying these parts off. Old wood may be brittle and split easily.

If it is not possible to remove the part, take exact measurements, make a drawing of what is to be made, and take that information with you to a woodworking shop. The replacement part should be of the same kind of wood as the original, so be sure you know what it is. It is best, but not mandatory, to use old wood for repairs, so check dealers' junk sections for wood for replacement parts.

Upholsterers are usually good about coming in to make an estimate. They will bring samples if you can give them some idea beforehand of what kind of fabric you want. But cash and carry is cheaper, so, again, take your furniture to the workshop if possible.

Many replacement parts can be bought readymade. These include:
Hardware (metal pulls, hooks, etc.)
Carved wooden pieces, including wooden drawer pulls,
   escutcheons (keyhole covers), fretwork
Fibreboard seats for chairs
Leather handles and other parts for trunks
Clock parts (frames and works)
Locks and keys
Lamp parts

If your antique dealer does not know of a local outlet, look through back issues of *The Antique Trader Weekly* until you find a firm that sells what you need. They don't all advertise every week, so you may have to scan several weeks' worth of newspapers.

You may want to replace old cane or fibreboard chair seats with new cane. There are a good many caning shops around where you can have this done. You may also do it yourself. It is not difficult, but it does require some time and patience, especially until you get the hang of it. Caning supplies, including kits for cane chair seats, can be bought through the mail from *Trader* advertisers. In larger cities there are often stores that sell caning supplies.

Mirrors and glass are another problem, but you get a replacement for a piece of broken glass the same way you get one for a broken wooden part. Mirrors that aren't broken can be resilvered, either by you (although it's a tricky chemical process) or a mirror shop. If all it needs is resilvering, it is much better to retain the old glass rather than buy new, but a *broken* mirror can be replaced without decreasing the furniture's antique value.

Examine the hinges. If they are bent, they can probably be taken off, straightened out, and put back. Sometimes hinges are loose merely because screws are loose or missing. If you want to use the old nail or screw holes, you can use slightly larger and/or longer nails or screws to secure a tight fit. My husband has developed an unusual method that works for him. He cuts off a couple of pieces of lead solder and puts them in the hole, then puts the nail or screw back in. Wooden matches, shim or wood dough can also be used as filler. These are all simple repairs that can greatly improve the function-ability of your antiques.

Some people make a big to-do about reusing original nails and screws. Sometimes this is possible, providing they can be straightened out and are not broken. But if using them will result in a shaky repair, discard them and use new ones. Handmade nails and screws are un-even and rough. Machine-made nails and screws are even and smooth. Although machine-made ones were available after mid-19th century, they were not always used, especially by country cabinetmakers, who may have continued to use up their stock of handmades for year after-ward. That's why the presence of handmade nails in a piece is not a reliable indicator of its age.

Drawers that stick or don't track correctly are annoying and keep people from enjoying the use of an antique. Take out the drawers, feel them and look at them. Often the edges are rough, a minor but im-portant defect that a little work with sandpaper can go a long way to correct. The same is true of the case the drawer slides into. Runners may have to be replaced or turned over. Dove-tailing may need reglu-ing. Some nails may have to be replaced. When these minor repairs are completed, rub soap or wax or use a silicone spray on the tracks and the drawer edges to make them slide freely. These procedures will probably cure 90 percent of drawer ills.

Examine the joints of your furniture. Are they loose? If so, you should reglue them. Carefully pry them slightly apart and check the dowels. If they are broken, that probably means a major repair. And, unless you are experienced, one that should be done in a woodworking shop.

If the dowels are in good shape, remove from the joints as much of the old glue as you can, by scraping or chipping or rubbing with steel wool. Apply wood glue to dowels and joints, clamp, and let dry. Since not much air can get into the joints during this process, the glue may take two or three times as long to dry as the directions say. If you unclamp too soon, the joints will come apart, and you will have to repeat the whole process. So let them dry a long time. Be careful also not to let new glue dry on the outside of the joint.

There are other products, not glues, for securing loose joints. These are liquid synthetics that swell the wood fibers, locking the joints in place. You may want to experiment with these products.

Remove the hardware from your acquisition and clean it. There are numerous chemical products that will do this job. Look for them in the furniture cleaner and polish section of hardware stores, antique stores, and in advertisements of trade publications. But sometimes chemical cleaners are not strong enough to clean furniture hardware. You may also have to use a wire wheel on an electric drill and/or steel wool. If a careless dealer has replaced hardware with brasses that are not of the same period as the originals, it is often possible to tell the shape of the original pulls by marks they have left on the fronts of drawers and doors. The very best replacements are antique brasses of the same period and style, but you may not want to go to the trouble of finding them. If not, there are two good alternatives: reproductions, and old brasses of the same period but a different style from the originals. As I have already mentioned, wooden reproductions, hand-carved or machine-made, are also available.

Now to the matter of refinishing. Actually, complete refinishing may not be necessary. Your piece may need nothing more than cleaning and polishing. Do not use soap and water. Mineral spirits or one of the new wood cleaners and feeders is generally a safe choice, but just to be sure you don't damage the present finish (if you want to retain it), test a small area on an underside to see how it reacts to the cleaner.

A favored oldtime finish was boiled linseed oil and turpentine, and it is still an easy and inexpensive way to bring life back to old wood. Buy the two ingredients at a hardware store and mix equal parts. Rub the mixture into the wood with a clean cloth. (Since oil causes wood, especially cherry, to darken, test it on an underside first.) Allow to dry. Wood that has been neglected for a long time may require two applications, with drying time in between. Finish with a paste wax made for furniture.

If, after you have cleaned the piece, it appears that there are several coats of paint or varnish, you may decide to remove some or all of them. There are several good paint and varnish removers on the market today. The product may be called a "stripper," and the process is called "stripping."

For stripping, you will need a ventilated work area, newspapers to cover the floor, medium to fine steel wool, rubber gloves, a putty knife, and a suede brush, a toothbrush, and cotton tips for getting into grooves. You will also need cotton and wool lint-free rags. Before scraping, file off the corners of your putty knife so that you cannot gouge the wood.

Follow carefully the directions for the specific product you use. They will differ in detail from those for other products. After removing the paint or varnish, you may want to smooth off the surface with fine sandpaper. Always rub with the grain. Don't sand away the blemishes that have accumulated over time—they're interesting. When you have finished stripping, your furniture should have none of the original or subsequent finishes remaining on it. You may have to go over the spots several times to be sure all of the previous finish is removed. Most of the stain may be gone, also. If you want to remove all of it, rub the piece with full-strength household bleach, and fine steel wool and allow to dry. Apply a filler if necessary.

Now, to bring out the beauty of the wood grain, stain the piece whatever shade you wish. Finally, apply a finishing coat—a varnish or a wax or an antique oil finish. The boiled linseed oil-turpentine mixture would be appropriate here also.

Stripping and refinishing a small table will take four or five hours of working time. Larger pieces, of course, will take longer. If stripping seems like too much work, or if your piece is intricately carved or has several layers of paint, you may choose to have the finish removed at a commercial stripping shop. Commercial stripping is relatively inexpensive, considering the amount of work it will save you. Chairs can be stripped for as little as $5; chests of drawers for $25-$30. The more time and care the piece requires, the higher the fee.

The strippers remove paint and varnish by hand or by dipping furniture in a chemical bath. Metal, including brass, wicker, and wooden furniture can be stripped in this manner. A valuable antique should not be dipped, nor should pieces that are veneered. Harsh chemicals sometimes raise the grain of the wood, oak in particular, making the surface rough, and you want to prevent that from happening. Dipping might also loosen joints. The stripper you consult should be able to advise you about whether it is safe to dip your piece.

The preferred method of restoring painted antiques is to preserve as much of the original paint as possible. The value of a piece will drop by 50 percent if you remove or cover up an original finish in good condition.

If the original paint is on the surface and at all presentable, merely clean up the piece, and protect the finish with shellac, lacquer, or varnish. You may want to apply a layer of paste wax as an added protection. A Hitchcock chair will look fine when "restored" in this way. Its painted decoration can be touched up with artist's oils before the clear finish is applied.

If the original paint is still there, but covered up with one or more layers of newer paint, you can, with care and a good paint remover, take off only the top layers. Try to remove only one layer at a time until the original paint is exposed.

Some old country pieces were painted with milk paint, a sour-milk concoction mixed with red or blue pigment. It is very difficult to remove, although it will come off with the help of ammonia. Use steel wool and rinse with water. Modern versions of milk paint are now being manufactured and you may want to refinish your country pieces with it. But, again, if the original milk-paint finish is at all presentable, don't remove it.

Fifty years ago, there was a craze for painting wood. In houses and apartments, fine old hardwood moldings and doors were painted over, and a lot of old furniture was painted over, too. In part, this was a reaction against the gloom of Victorian interiors; in part it was a method of covering up inferior or mixed woods of new products.

Now, there is a mania for stripping wood. It's true that stripping and refinishing often reveals interesting and beautiful markings in the wood, but refinishing everything in the same way produces a certain sameness, too. Each piece of furniture should be considered as an individual and handled in that manner. An acquaintance of mine who collects spinning wheels says that the more she learns about antiques, the less she wants to do to them. I think that's the best approach. After all, isn't a chipped and worn original at least as interesting as a slicked-up version?

Introduction to State Directory

In nearly every small town in the Midwest, there is an antique shop. Not all of them are listed here. The list is made up of antique dealers about whom I felt I had sufficient information. There is more information about some than others; each listing contains all that I know about each establishment. I have included some of what I consider incomplete listings because those dealers stock unusual or particularly interesting merchandise or because they are in sparsely settled areas that I felt should be represented. I have not knowingly included any shop that does not carry furniture, though I have included quite a few whose primary interest is not furniture, but who do sell it.

I have not, of course, personally visited every shop in the list. I gathered the information for the list by checking advertisements in antique trade publications, contacting state and local tourist agencies and chambers of commerce, culling names and addresses from telephone directories, excerpting material from my own notes and memory, and nagging knowledgeable friends and strangers. The number of antique shops in large cities is staggering, and I have chosen only a few in each city to be included in this directory. My theory is that if you are in a large city, you can easily check the telephone directory yourself and pick out a few dealers who seem to carry the kind of antiques you are interested in and/or are in geographic areas accessible to you. I have included proportionally more small-town or country shops, because I think they are harder to locate. N.A.D.A. in a dealer listing means "member of National Antique Dealers Association;" C.A.D.A. means "Canadian Antique Dealers Association."

Antique shops, like other small businesses, appear and vanish with disconcerting unpredictability, and antique dealers are independent types who just might decide to go fishing for the day rather than keep the shop open. For these reasons, I strongly urge you to telephone any shop you plan to visit to be sure they will be open at a particular time. I have had too many experiences of driving miles to an out-of-the-way shop only to find the front door locked. I don't want you to have a similar experience.

Dealers are listed by towns, which are in alphabetical order by state. If you want to locate shops in a particular area that might include several towns, look through the listing for all the shops that have telephone numbers that begin with the area code assigned to that area. For example, if I am going to be traveling through Madison, Wisconsin, I would look through the Wisconsin listing for all the shops that have the Madison area code (608) in their phone number. Except for the big cities, towns that have a number of antique shops are generally richer in antiques than the average. An unusual number of shops in a small town—20 or 30, for instance—is an indication that antiques and tourism is the principal business of the town.

If you are particularly pleased or particularly displeased by any of the shops listed, or if the listing includes misinformation, I would much appreciate your writing to tell me about it. And the same holds true if you know of shops that should be listed and are not.

Renewed interest in Midwest antiques is part of a general and growing enthusiasm for Midwest history. In every state, there are restored houses, restored villages, and historical museums that bring us one step closer to understanding life in the 19th-century Midwest. You may want to combine antique shopping with visits to historical sites and restorations. Check with state and local tourism bureaus for up-to-date information.

Illinois

Prime antique-shopping areas in Illinois include Galena, in the northwest corner of the state; Richmond, near the Illinois-Wisconsin line northwest of Chicago; and Rossville, 100 miles south of Chicago. Galena's "season" is May to November, so check with dealers to be sure their shops will be open during your visit. Several times a year, there are tours and open houses in Galena. Check with the chamber of commerce for current information. Bishop Hill, site of a Swedish settlement, and Nauvoo, site of a Mormon settlement, offer museums and restorations to visitors interested in Midwest history and furniture. The Chicago Historical Society's bicentennial exhibition, featuring Chicago life in the period 1885-1925, will evolve into permanent displays, including furniture made in that period.

Algonquin, Illinois

The Fox's Den
Cliff and Betty Skoog
Antique furniture
975 N. Harrison St. 60102
312/658-8198 by appointment

Alton, Illinois

The Gray Barn
B. Flactiff and D. Hawkins
1610 Henry St. 52002
618/465-8165
Closed Tuesdays

Beardstown, Illinois

Iva and Rudy's Antiques
615 Edwards 62618
217/323-4344
Open 9 to 9

Belleville, Illinois

Antiques by Elaine Matthews
510 Freeburg Ave. 62221
Shop: 618/234-5122
Home: 618/538-7403
Open by chance or appointment
N.A.D.A.

Belvidere, Illinois

Pheasant Hill Antiques
Harold and Ruth Luhman
Rt. 3, Box 46
North of Belvidere on Hwy. 76 to
  Squaw Prairie Rd. Turn right
  (east). Go to second crossroad, turn
  left on Grange Hall Rd., ½ mi. to a
  lane, turn right.
815/547-6793

Bement, Illinois

Olde Keeping Room
Bernice Goodmon
Primitives, small wood items, old
  pine, copper, brass
2 mi. south, 4½ mi. east of
  Bement, R.R. 1 61813
217/678-8350
By appointment only

Bloomington, Illinois

Candlelight Antiques
Chuck and Louise Young
General line, furniture, art and
  pattern glass, china, jewelry
1102 E. Oakland
309/829-2653

Mary Bell Antiques
Marie Bishop
Furniture, china, glass, appraisals,
  estate sales
2405 S. Main St.
309/829-6497
Open 7 days, 1 to 5

Prather's
Ethel Prather
General line, furniture, china,
  glassware
311 E. Baker St.
309/828-9257

Red Door Antiques
Sam Ramsey and Bob Lewis
Furniture, primitives, china, glass
1102 E. Oakland Ave.
309/829-2653

Yarger's Antiques
Mrs. Jess Yarger
General line, clocks, glass
912 S. Summit St.
309/829-9011

Canton, Illinois

Flahavin Antiques
China, glass, furniture, primitives
1 block west of South Main on West
  Walnut
309/647-0818

Carthage, Illinois

Heirloom Antiques and Fine Gifts
Mr. and Mrs. Carl Geissler
Clocks, glass, china, general line.
  Indian turquoise and silver
Hwy. 136 in Carthage
Open Mon. thru Sat. 10 to 5:30
Sun., 1 to 5, or by appointment
Shop: 217/357-2632
Home: 217/357-3408

Champaign, Illinois

Antiques
Jean and Ernie Mehnert
Furniture, china, glass,
  miscellaneous
819 W. Washington St. 61820
217/352-3844
By chance or appointment

Charleston, Illinois

Fireside Antiques
Fred and Jackie Moler
General line, furniture, china, glass
R.R. 3, 6 mi. north on Rt. 130
 61920
217/345-3619
Mon. thru Fri. 10 to 10
Sat. & Sun. 12 to 6

Chicago, Illinois

Harrison-Davis Trading Co., Inc.
George Harrison Daniels,
Judy Davis Thornber
Antiques, primitives, accessories
2423 N. Clark St. 60614
312/750-7355, 549-2940
Open 7 days, 11 to 9

Hollywood Art Galleries
6618 N. Ridge Rd., 60626
Buyers, sellers and consignees of
 fine furniture, bric-a-brac, objects
 of art, collector plates
312/743-3573

Russ's Pier W
Antiques, oil paintings, furniture
2823 N. Lincoln, 12 to 10
1227 W. Diversey, 12 to 4:30
312/327-5718

Victorian House Antiques
806 W. Belmont
312/348-8561
Open 7 days, 24-hr. service

Cissna Park, Illinois

Unique Antiques
Norman Maul
1 mi. west of Cissna Park or 7 mi.
 east Rt. I-57
815/457-2435
By appointment only

Columbia, Illinois

Town & Country Antiques
610 S. Main St.
Glassware and furniture
618/281-4191
Mon. thru Thurs., Sat. 9 to 5
Fridays 'til 8:30

Congerville, Illinois

Norris' Antiques
Beulah Norris
General line, primitives, glassware
309/448-2288

Danville, Illinois

Country Store Antiques
Vic and Florence Gony
Primitives, china, jewelry, furniture
3607 N. Vermilion Rt. 1 North 61832
217/442-8897

Nightlinger's
Antiques and collectibles
106 Greenwood Ave. Rt. 1 South
217/446-5129
10 to 6 Tues., Thurs., Sat., Sun.

Decatur, Illinois

The Browse Shop
Creola Pribble, Carole and
  Margarette Meisenheimer
General line
R.R. 2, Box 289, Rock Springs
217/423-9884

Cellar Antiques
Jim and Irene Kueper
General line, primitives, glassware
2720 E. Hickory 62521
217/423-4682
By chance or appointment

The Shelf Shop
Gypsy and Ed Redmond
2 mi. east of Airport Rd. on Rt. 36
Box 112, R.R. 7   62521
217/864-2643

Downers Grove, Illinois

Troika Antiques
433 Ogden Ave. 60515
312/964-6144; 832-1467

El Paso, Illinois

Helen's Antique & Resale Shop
Helen Scott
General line, furniture, jewelry
546 Elmwood Ct. 61738
309/0447

Elizabeth, Illinois

Little Barn Antiques
Bill and Betty Boekhaus
Furniture and general line
Terrapin Ridge-Derinda Rd., ¼ mi.
  south of Rt. 20
815/858-2037

Elliott, Illinois

DFK Stembel Antiques
60933
217/749-2236
Sat., Sun., Mon. afternoons or by
  appointment

Eureka, Illinois

The Old Shop
Antiques and rare books
108 East Center 61530
309/467-3613

Farmer City, Illinois

Alexander's Antiques
Howard Alexander
General line, furniture, glassware,
  jewelry
Rt. 54, 152 Clinton Ave. 61842
217/928-9691

Flossmoor, Illinois

H.L. Enterprises Co.
Henry B. Leopold
Estate sales, auctions, appraisals
1630 Holbrook Rd. 60422
312/798-7066

Frankfort, Illinois

Allen's Antiques
Appraisals, auction service available
100 Kansas St.
Shop: 815/469-5535
Home: 312/748-6064
Closed Mon.

Freeport, Illinois

E.W. Pyfer
Specializing in lamps and lighting
   fixtures
218 N. Foley Ave. 61032
815/232-8968
By appointment only

Galena, Illinois

Bartsch's Antiques & Lamp Hospital
Mr. and Mrs. Del Bartsch
Lamps, glass, china. Lamp mounting
   and wiring a specialty
408 Washington St.
Open year round

Bless This Mess Antiques
Mr. and Mrs. D. Miller
General line
101 N. Main St.
Open year round

*Brown Beaver Antiques &
Collectibles*
General line, collector's items
116 N. Main St.
Open weekends

*Carriage House Antiques & Guest
House*
Mary Keller Lombardi
Furniture, glass, china, silver
1004 Park Ave. (east end of bridge)
Open year round

The Gazebo
Charles Marston
Antiques, et cetera
222 S. Main St.
Open June thru September, other
   times by appointment

Glick's Antiques
Eldon Glick
General line
112 N. Main
815/777-0781
Open year round

Harvey Antiques
Harvey Pranian
Antiques, handcrafted and antique
   jewelry
220 N. Main St.
Open May thru Oct.

Helen's Country Cupboard
Helen Wirth
General line of antiques, handmade
   candles
304 S. Main St.
Open daily during season

Mansion Antiques
Wm. C. Barrett
Furniture, lamps, clocks and clock
  repair
214 S. Main St.
Open year round

Ra Ho Antiques
G. Rank
Radios, photographs, furniture,
  general line
114 N. Main St.
Open year round

Seminary Antiques
Mr. and Mrs. Frank Kendrick
General line
226 N. Bench St.
Open summer and fall

Shop of Memories
Leonard Goedkin, Jr.
Furniture, dishes, lamps
244 N. Main St.
Open year round

Stagecoach Stop Antiques
Paul Goedkin
Brass beds, furniture, dishes
245 N. Main St.
Open year round

The Stone Mill, Inc.
J. LaRocco and J. Mead
Furniture and fine antiques
324 Spring St.
Open summer and fall

Victorian Antique Shop
Mr. and Mrs. M. Sitzman
Victorian antiques a specialty
Hwy. 20 W. across from Palace
  Motel
Open year round

Virginia's Antiques
Virginia Fitzgerald
Primitives, pine and pottery
301 S. Main St.
Open year round

The White House
413 S. Prospect
Galena's oldest antique shop

Geneva, Illinois

House of Antiques
18th and early 19th century American furniture, primitives
314 E. State St. 60134
312/232-9650
N.A.D.A.

Gilman, Illinois

Shirley Ryan's Antiques
Shirley Stevenson Ryan
General line and jewelry
815/265-7256

Grayslake, Illinois

*Grayslake Fairgrounds Antiques
  Market*
40 mi. north of Chicago 3 mi. west of
  I94 on Rt. 45
414/563-4396
2nd and usually 4th Sun. 9 to 5

Hainesville, Illinois

The Country Boutique
Barbara Bonde
Rt. 120 and Hainesville Rd., P.O.
  Box 153, Grayslake, IL
312/BA 3-2452; KI 6-4295
7 days, 11 to 5, or by appointment

Hanover Park, Illinois

Culverwell Antiques
Furniture, clocks, auto parts
2015 Lake St. (Rt. 20) 60103
312/289-2360

Harrisburg, Illinois

Pavey's Antiques
Mrs. Bonnie Pavelonis
General line
1265 S. Granger St. 62946
618/252-3435
After 5 p.m. weekdays; 10 to 5
  weekends

Heyworth, Illinois

Weathervane Antiques
Charles and Verla Hamilton
Furniture, primitives, glassware
110 Sullivan St. & Rt. 51 61745
309/473-2468

Hoopeston, Illinois

Oyler's Antiques
Margaret and Clair Oyler
Furniture, art and pattern glass,
  coins, books
R.R. 3 W. Thompson Ave. 60942
217/283-7233

Jacksonville, Illinois

Vickie's Antiques
Mrs. C. William Ator
Furniture, primitives, glassware,
  china, jewelry
1050 W. College
217/245-6706

Joliet, Illinois

Beacon Trading Post
Don Bumgarner
New and used furniture, antiques
305 Willow Ave. 60436
815/722-8125

Olde Time Shoppe
The Steinquists
Antiques, clocks, collectibles
430 Jessie St. 60433
815/727-9173; 723-1935
By chance or appointment

Kewanee, Illinois

Antiques
Keith Parker
Old tools, primitives, collectibles
111 W. 13th St. 61443
309/853-4664

McMillan's Antiques
Minette McMillan
General line
693 N. Main St. 61443
309/853-8798

Lebanon, Illinois

Poverty Hollow Antiques
Georgia Halmsey
Furniture, glassware, primitives
4/10 mi. north of Horner Park
R.R. 1, Box 63 62254
618/537-2243
Open noon to dark

Lincoln, Illinois

Red Barn Antiques
Ed and Gladys Browning
Stripping and refinishing
114 S. Chicago St.
217/732-2523
Closed Thurs., Sun.

Lockport, Illinois

Pilgrim Hall
Antique mall featuring 8 dealers
10th and Hamilton 60441
815/838-0435
7 days, 12-5

Macomb, Illinois

Stone House Antiques
Verda and Kimbrough Shake
Walnut and pine furniture, primitives, lamps
614 W. Murray St.
309/833-5362

McLean, Illinois

Puffabelly Station
Rebecca Beeler and Carol Lystad
General line
Rt. 136 north of "Dixie"
309/874-3161

McLeansboro, Illinois

Melba's Antiques
General line, no reproductions
601 S. Washington St. 62859
618/643-3355
Closed Tues.

Milledgeville, Illinois

G.L. Stanley, Antiquarian
8,000 sq. ft. on Hwy. 88
2 East 8th St.
815/225-7239

Monee, Illinois

Monee Antique Mall
Kitty and Ray Kiefer
Manhattan-Monee Rd. 60449
312/563-2770

Monroe Center, Illinois

Detig's Antiques
Robert and Becky Detig
2 mi. north of Monroe Center 61052
815/393-4337
By chance or appointment

Mt. Olive, Illinois

Chalice Antique Shoppe
Skip and Mary Jane Hastings
310 W. First South
217/999-7519
Closed Thurs. Mon. thru Sat. 9 to 5
Sun. 11 to 5

Naperville, Illinois

Barnick's Antiques
1850 House
Antiques, dolls, toys, old-fashioned
candy store
509 W. Aurora Ave. (Rt. 65) 60540
312/420-2780
Tues. thru Fri. 12 to 3
Sat. & Sun. 12 to 5

Oak Lawn, Illinois

The Browsatorium
Hilda M. Breuer
9505 S. Cook Ave. 60453
312/423-8955

Oak Park, Illinois

Aunt Teak's Memory Lane
Dia Walsh, Shelly Weiser
130 N. Ridgeland 60302
312/386-9842
Tues. thru Sat. 11 to 6

Odin, Illinois

Lincoln Trail Antiques
Pauline, Gay and Jim Soper
Across from water tower on Hwy. 50
   62870
618/775-8255; 775-6173
7 days, 8 to 6

Old Town Antiques
Sam and Louise Davidson
Old things and estates bought and
   sold.
Main St. (Res: 155 Clinmar,
   Centralia)
Shop: 618/775-7360
Home: 618/532-6477

Orland Park, Illinois

General Store
16 dealers, 2 floors
14314 Union, near I-80
   Rts. 294, 55, 57
312/349-0313
Open 7 days

Ottawa, Illinois

Ray Burke's Antiques
Ray and Beth Burke
Furniture, lamps, china, glassware
1323 W. LaFayette St. 61350
851/433-2340

Pana, Illinois

Lucille's Antiques
Mrs. Merle Drain
Furniture, glass, china, lamps
E. 4th and Vine 62557
217/562-5228
By chance or appointment

Pekin, Illinois

Andy's Antiques
Rex E. and Bernice E. Andrews
General line, glassware
1308 Willow 61554
309/346-0173

Fran's Antiques
Frances Mickle
General line, primitives, glass, china
1217 State St. 61554
309/346-0703
By chance or appointment

Louise Kennelley Antiques
Louise Kennelley
Primitives, glassware, china
1402 North 4❂ 61554
309/346-6066
By appointment only

Peoria, Illinois

Alberta's Antiques
Kurt and Alberta Leucht
General line, china
1708 S. Arago St. 61605
309/637-2156

B & M Antiques
Bernard E. Harding and E.F.
   McHugh
General line
1600 W. Kettelle St.
309/676-1000

Spruce Acres Antiques
Mildred Birwin
General line
1514 E. Garden Lane 61614
Off Galena Rd. — Forest Park Dr.
309/685-7315

Pittsfield, Illinois

Midway Antiques No. 2
Gene and Shirley Johns
Furniture, glass, china, primitives,
  Indian relics, old bottles, jars
217/285-4831; 734-2010

Pontiac, Illinois

Bill O'Brien Antiques
William O'Brien
General line, glassware
201 N. Mill St. 61764
815/844-6078

Pontiac, Illinois

Peg's Antique Lamp Painting
Peg Grotevant
Shades painted to match antique
  bases
610 W. Henry St. 61764
By appointment only

Princeton, Illinois

House of the Past
Eleanor and Herman Husser
Furniture, glassware, china, pictures
209 Park Ave. West
815/872-7562
By chance or appointment

Quincy, Illinois

The Den of Antiquity
Frances G. Castle
General line antiques
427 S. 7th St. 62301
217/223-8929

Raleigh, Illinois

Wagon Wheel Antiques
1 mi. east of Raleigh, 3 mi. west of
  Eldorado 62977
618/273-9282
Open 7 days

Rantoul, Illinois

Weathervane Antiques
C.P. Hamiltons
Primitives, furniture, china, glass
317 E. Wabash 61866
217/893-9414

Richmond, Illinois

Carpenter & Smith
Restoration
10310½ Main St.
815/678-4245

Corner Store
Furniture, etc.
10315 Main St.
815/678-4214
Daily 8 to 5

The Country Place
Furniture, decorative accessories
5601 Broadway St.
815/678-4311; 338-5562
  11 to 5 except closed Mon. & Fri.

Ed's Antiques
Furniture, etc.
10321 Main St.
815/678-2911
Mon. thru Sat. 10 to 5
Sun. 11 to 5

Happy House
General antiques
5604 Broadway St.
815/678-4082

J & E Emporium
Antiques, clocks, coins
10331 Main St.
815/678-4441

Little Bit Antiques
5603 Broadway St.
815/678-4218
Daily 10:30 to 5

Pennebaker's Antiques
General line and dolls
5626 Broadway St.
815/678-7611
Daily 10:30 to 5

Serendipity Shop
General antiques and furniture
9818 Main St.
815/678-4141
  Daily 10 to 5

Suzie's Antiques
General, glass, china, pottery
10331 Main St.
815/678-4337
10:30 to 5 daily

Village Trader
Traditional and primitive antiques
5608 Broadway St.
815/678-4259
Sat. & Sun. 10 to 5

Rochester, Illinois

Helen's Antiques
General line, furniture, china, glass
R.R. 2, Oakhill Rd. 62563
217/637-7416
By chance or appointment

Roseville, Illinois

Copper Kettle
Paul and Audrey Stevens
Furniture, primitives, china,
  collectibles
61473
309/426-2043
Sat. and by appointment

Rossville, Illinois

100 miles south of Chicago
Approximately 30 shops along
  Chicago Ave. (State Route #1) and
  Attica St.

Rushville, Illinois

Trone's Antiques
Furniture, primitives, glass, china,
  collectibles
114 N. Congress
217/322-3127; 322-6125

Sparta, Illinois

Collectors Corner
Gene and Ruth Hicks
501 E. Main St. 62286
618/443-3275
Tues. thru Sun. 10:30 to 7

Springfield, Illinois

Murray's Oxbow Antiques
W. Jerome and Helen T. Murray
Small pieces of furniture, primitives,
  china, glass, pictures
2509 Whittier Ave. 62704
217/528-8220

Watson's Antiques
General line, glassware, sterling
48 Cheyenne Dr. 62704
217/546-0201

Ye Olden Days Antiques
John and Barbara Bensi
General line, china, glass
2300 E. Sangamon 62702
217/544-2691

Stewardson, Illinois

Heidi's Antiques
Mary Vonderheide
Furniture, glass, primitives,
  collectibles
302 W. South Fourth 62463
217/682-3627
By chance or appointment

Sullivan, Illinois

The Depot
General line, china, glassware
6 mi. out on West Eden Rd., R.D. 4
P.O. Box 137 61951
217/797-6445

Trenton, Illinois

Iron Gate Antiques
David and Judy Stepp
Furniture, glassware, crockery,
  lamps, toys, telephones
221 W. Second
618/224-7113

Urbana, Illinois

Wantland's Antiques
Ralph and Virginia Wantland
General line, china, glass, silver
604 W. Vermont 61801
217/344-5315
By chance or appointment

Vandalia, Illinois

Odds N Ends Antiques
Lida M. Hale
Furniture, clocks, china, glass
1309 W. Tower St. 11 blocks west of
  Old State Capitol, follow Rt. 140
  to sign
618/283-0158

Washington, Illinois

Mary Rachel Antique Shop
Mary and Harold Levery
General line
501 Walnut St. Rt. 24
309/283-2911

Watseka, Illinois

Mahlon and Betty Williams
Mahlon and Betty Williams
Furniture, lamps, refinishing and
restoration
315 E. Mulberry
815/432-4395

Wayne City, Illinois

The Shed of Antiques
Betty Rosenburgh
Furniture, china, pottery, glassware,
 collectibles
62895
618/895-2810

Wenona, Illinois

Hoge's Antiques
Josephine and Leroy Hoge
General line
Downtown Wenona 61377
815/853-4503; 853-4686

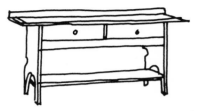

Westmont, Illinois

Col. Danhelka's Antiques & Co.
Antique store, auction service
7 W. Quincy 60559
312/971-2522; 325-0107; 654-2623
Daily 10-10 or appointment

West Union, Illinois

Bette's Antique Shop
Bette A. Strohm
Furniture, china, general line
R.R. 1 62477
217/279-3307

Wilmette, Illinois

May West Locke
Antiques, collecting and shopping
 service
2041 Wilmette Ave. 60091
312/AL 6-0816
By chance or appointment

Woodbine, Illinois

Glick's Antiques
Eldon Glick
General line
20 mi. east of Galena on U.S. 20

Wonder Lake, Illinois

Wondermere Farm Antiques
Elda Mansmith
9111 Wondermere Rd. 60097
815/653-7497
Generally open, but appointment
 suggested

Indiana

Each year in Goshen in northern Indiana, 160 Mennonite church communities sponsor the Michiana Mennonite Relief Sale. It happens on a Saturday at the end of September, beginning with a sausage and pancake breakfast, continuing with the quilt auction, the used items sale, and the antique auction. There's a sneak preview the evening before. More than 20,000 people went last year to eat homecooked food and buy up antiques and handcrafted items. The fair is held at the 4-H Fairgrounds one mile east of Goshen, just off US Highway 33. Check with the Goshen chamber of commerce for information on the fair and accommodations.

Anderson, Indiana

Brocantell
Norma Collings
3316 Boulevard Way   46011
317/642-7561

The Coach Light
Roberta Burke
General line
1501 W. 53rd St. 46011
317/643-4021
By chance or appointment

The Golden Trashery
303 W. 14th 46011
317/643-3200

Angola, Indiana

Red Barn Antiques
Antiques and unusual gifts
3 mi. west of I-69 on U.S. 20
219/665-6818
Memorial Day - Labor Day
(Winter location: 3205 N. Wells, Ft.
  Wayne, 219/483-7149)

Arlington, Indiana

Nelson's Antiques
Mr. and Mrs. Joel Hadley
46104
317/663-2492

Attica, Indiana

Bonnie's Bygones
Furniture, glassware, primitives
Rt. 2 47918
5 mi. northeast of Attica, turn west
  at West Point on Co. Rd. 510S.
317/572-2527

Brazil, Indiana

Crestline Antiques
General line antiques
531 E. National St.
812/442-1061
Open daily 10 to 3

Bremen, Indiana

Roy and Ron's Antiques
General line antiques, furniture,
  china
116 S. Marshall St., ½ block off
  Rt. 6   46506
219/546-3212
9 to 4:30; Sun. 1:30 to 4:30

Bristol, Indiana

Nancy Foster's Antique Store

The Old Store Antique Shop

Sugar 'n Spice Antique Shop

Cambridge City, Indiana

Huddleston House Inn
Pat Steele Antiques
Country furniture and accessories
Hwy. 40 West
317/478-2251
By appointment

Centerville, Indiana

Alcorn Antiques
General line, specializing in quilts
214 W. Main
317/855-3161

American House Antiques
General line, furniture, quality glass
101 W. Main
Open daily

Custer's Antiques
General line, furniture
207 E. Main
317/855-3521
Open daily

Bob Dafler
"The smallest shop in Centerville"
109 S. Morton Ave.
317/855-5532

Twin Pines
Ken and Kathy Musselman
401 N. Morton
317/855-2777
Open daily

Verlon Webb
Exclusive line
510 N. Morton
317/855-5542
Appointment suggested

Webb's Antiques
Ellis Webb
General line antiques
311 E. Main 47330
317/855-2282
Open 7 days

Chesterfield, Indiana

Harry's Country Auction
Bethany Church Rd.
317/378-7924

Chesterton, Indiana

The Antique Shop
Porter Ave. and Calumet Rd.
219/926-1400
Weekdays 10 to 5
Sun. 12 to 6

Chesterton, Indiana

Carol's Antiques
119 Broadway (across from park)
219/926-4757
Open 7 days 10 to 5

The Freight Station
Antiques, tearoom, plants and
  gallery
Tues. thru Sat. 10 to 5
Sun. 12 to 5

Tree House Antiques
Country pieces
3 mi. east of Hwy. 49 on Hwy. 20
Tues. thru Sun. 1 to 4:30

Columbia City, Indiana

Marion's Yesterday Shop
Antiques and collectibles
410 E. Jefferson St. 46725
7 days, 9 to 6

Corydon, Indiana

Miller's Antiques
Mr. and Mrs. J.P. Miller
Hwy. 460, 4 mi. west first cross road,
  south 1 mi. 47112
812/738-32860
Open 7 days

Decatur, Indiana

Town House
Paul and Patricia Morgan
General line, clocks
222 N. 2nd St. 46733
219/724-2920
Weekdays 1 to 9; Sat. 9 to 9
Closed Sun.

Eaton, Indiana

Heirloom Antiques
Mrs. Ina Loughmiller
301 N. Hartford St. 47338
317/396-3472
Daily 8 to 8 except Wed., Sun.

English, Indiana

Mary's Antiques
Mary Williams
R.R. 1 47118
812/338-2061
Daily 'til 7:30 p.m.

Evansville, Indiana

The Antique Corner
Furniture, china, glassware, paintings, collectibles
211 W. Jennings
812/853-5236

Frontier Traders Antiques
Primitives, one of a kind
1151 Diamond Ave.
812/425-7069

Fremont, Indiana

The Barnstable Antique Shop
Country furniture and miscellany
2 mi. west of Fremont or ½ mi. east
  of Jct. I-69 and Indiana toll road,
on State Rd. 120
219/495-5875

Gene's Antique Shop
Gene Norton
General line antiques
"One of Indiana's largest"
N. Pleasant
219/495-9982; 675-9876

Greentown, Indiana

Ruth's Antiques
General line, orientals
502 W. Main
317/628-3895
By chance or appointment

Hartford City, Indiana

Little Colonial Shoppe
Ethelmae and Floyd Hahn
Antiques, glass, china, gifts
220½ W. Water St. 47348
317/348-1439

Highland, Indiana

The Green Apple Antiques
Pat Moore
American antiques: furniture,
  copper, brass, china, jewelry,
  accessories
3833 Ridge Rd. 46322
Tues. thru Sat. 10 to 5

Huntington, Indiana

B'Naddie's Junque Shoppe
815 Poplar St. 46750
219/356-0886

Huntington, Indiana

Wells Variety Barn
Helen Wells
General line
5 mi. south of Huntington, Rts. 9
  and 37
219/468-2020

Indianapolis, Indiana

Irving What Not Shop
Ross and Helen Sheets
Antiques and gifts, appraisals
6017 E. Washington St. 46219
317/356-5570

Traylor's Antique Flea Market
Leo and Laura Taylor
50 dealers, 12,000 sq. ft.
7159 E. 46th St.
Sat. & Sun. 9 to 6

Jeffersonville, Indiana

Clark County Auction
1031 S. Clark Blvd.
call 812/282-7805 for information

Kokomo, Indiana

Hill's Studio
Joseph Michalski
Furniture, china, glassware, pre-1940
  toys, banks, trains
124 W. Walnut
317/457-2972
Daily 9:30 to 5:30 except Sun.
By chance or appointment

Lafayette, Indiana

Antiques & Stamps
Iona and Walter Wulff
General line
1731 Morton St.
317/742-2646

Liberty Center, Indiana

Gaiser's Antiques
Mr. and Mrs. Carl Gaiser
R.R. 1   46776
Daily 12 to 5

Lowell, Indiana

Lor Jon Gifts and Antiques
E.J. Zunica
Antiques, Indian jewelry, gifts
201 Commercial Ave. 46356
219/696-6788

Madaryville, Indiana

Frank & Helen's Shop
Mr. and Mrs. Frank Haskins
Box 41   47957
Mon., Wed., Fri., Sat. 10 to 6

Merrilville, Indiana

Putman's
Richard and Lois Putman
Antiques, odds and ends
7103 Taft St. 46410
219/769-8398

Metamora, Indiana

The Et Cetera Shop
On U.S. 52
513/893-1577
May thru Nov., Sun. only

Mishawaka, Indiana

LaCave Antiques
Fine antiques and unusual
  collectibles; appraisal service at
  home or in the shop
100 Center Complex (in the basement
  of The Brewery)
219/259-6943
Daily 10 to 9 except Sun. 12 to 6

The Stable
Large selection of antiques and
  collectibles
100 Center Complex (in the Old
  Kamm's Brewery)
219/255-0500
Open on weekends only

Monon, Indiana

Overley's Antiques
Furniture, primitives, lamps, clocks,
    glass, china
500 N. Market St. 47959
219/253-6460

Nappanee, Indiana

Unsicker Antiques
Furniture, depression glass
U.S. 6, 1 block east of St. Rd. 19
Open 9 to 5 except Tues. and Wed.
    by chance

Nashville, Indiana

Alberts Mall
1¼ mi. southwest on St. Rd. 46 (near
entrance to Brown County State
Park) Several dealers, opening April
1, 1976
Open 6 days, April thru Dec.
For information, call Alberts
Antiques, Goodland, Indiana
219/297-3293

New Albany, Indiana

State Street Used Furniture
529 State
812/944-4849

The Treasure House of Antiques
1524 E. Market
812/944-4860

New Harmony, Indiana

Heart of Harmony Antiques
Furniture, glass, china, collectibles
510 S. Main
812/682-4468

Newburgh, Indiana

The Corner
Eleanor Rehmel, Edie Wallenbrook
211 W. Jennings St.
812/853-5236

Pierceton, Indiana

Country Lane Antiques
C.R. Oxenrider
P.O. Box 206 46562
State Rd. 13, 4 mi. north of
    US 30

Plymouth, Indiana

B & B Antiques & Used Furniture
Country antiques
1000 W. Jefferson
219/936-3685
Daily 9 to 5 except Sun. 1 to 5

Georgia C. Boggs
Furniture, glass, china, miscel-
    laneous ("large stock")
1½ mi. north of Holiday Inn on old
    U.S. 31, east side
R.R. 1 46563
219/936-2619

Plymouth, Indiana

The Hanger
William A. Hopkins
Antiques, Collectibles, furniture
  stripping
R.R. 7, Box 116A 46563
U.S. 30 W.
219/936-9017; 936-6607

Rockville, Indiana

Covered Bridge Antiques
Mr. and Mrs. John Adams
46872
812/569-5339
9 to 5 weekdays; Sun. 12 to 5

Seelyville, Indiana

Knotty Pine Antique Shop
General line antiques
Specializing in antique oil lamps
  and repair
5 mi. east of Terre Haute on US 40
812/877-9209

Shipshewana, Indiana

Rainbow Arts and Crafts
Leonard and Lois Haarer
Antiques, crafts
46565
Home: 219/768-4590

South Bend, Indiana

Thieves Market
45 permanent shops of antiques,
  original art, handcrafts
2309 E. Edison (½ block east of
  Ironwood)
219/233-9820
Open Sat. and Sun. only, 10 to 6

Stilesville, Indiana

Hartman's Antiques and Gifts
Roy and Edna Hartman
North side of Rt. 40 at stop and go
  signals
Box 213 46180
317/539-6032

Swayzee, Indiana

Sprinkle's Antiques
Furniture, collectibles, gifts
403 N. Washington St. 46986
317/922-7185

Terre Haute, Indiana

Aardvark Valley Antiques
General line, furniture
817 Crawford, 7 blocks south of
  Civic Center
812/234-2250
Daily-evenings

The Attic
Antiques, furniture, used furniture
"Trash to treasures"
2511 S. Third, 6 blocks north of
  I-70 on US 41
812/232-8606
10 to dusk except Mon.

Martin's Antiques
Furniture, primitives, glass, china,
  lamps, appraisals
1605 S. Seventh 47802
812/232-8756

Revival Antiques
Betty Ann Kraly, Don L. Mercer
General line antiques, art, gifts
1322 S. Eleventh 47802
812/232-4720

Swank, William L.
Specializing in furniture and clocks
Mainly wholesale
1119 N. Eighth 47802
812/235-7734
By chance or appointment

Valparaiso, Indiana

Uphaus Antique Shop
Stony Hills Farm
Henry and Leona Uphaus
Furniture, dishes
RFD 6, 46883
Turn west ½ mi. at road marker 100,
south on St. Rd. 2
219/462-2810
9 to 5 except closed Sun.

Walton, Indiana

Old Sawmill Flea Market & Auction
US Hwy. 35 South
219/626-2713

 Iowa

Although there weren't nearly as many furnituremakers in Iowa as in some of the other Midwestern states, the state seems to have ended up with a lot of furniture and is dotted with interesting antique shops. In northern Iowa shoppers looking for furniture, primitives, and art glass will be interested in antique shops in Belmond, Bolan, Charles City, Kensett, Manly, Mason City, Rockford, Osage, Sheffield, and Stacyville.

Aplington, Iowa

Ray King's Antiques &
Organic Foods
Furniture, primitives, clocks,
 glassware, china, watches
50604
319/347-2752; 347-6260

Atkins, Iowa

Lorraine's Antiques
Primitives, furniture, glass, lamps
208 First Ave. 52206
319/446-3783

Auburn, Iowa

Lois's Antiques
P.O. Box F 51433
Near the water tower in Auburn
712/688-2279

Belle Plaine, Iowa

Main Street USA Antiques
Carolyn Wells
"Antiques of quality"
7th Ave. and 12th St. 52208

Bellevue, Iowa

Cart-tique Cellar
Joan Wagner
Antiques, gifts, glassware,
 handiwork
9 mi. north of Bellevue off Hwy. 52
319/872-4930
Daily from 1 to 7; Sat. & Sun., 1 to 6

Belmond, Iowa

Henn's Scratch 'n Find
Primitives, furniture, collector's
 items
4 mi. south on Hwy. 69, 1 ⅓ mi.
 east
515/444-8297
Summer: 9 to 5; also by chance or
 appointment

Bolan, Iowa

Bolan Store
General line antiques
5 mi. east of Hwy. 65 at Kensett, then
 1 mi. north, ¼ mi. east
515/845-2252
Mon.-Sat. 8 to 6
Sun. by chance

Calamus, Iowa

The Depot
Noel Olson, Lyle Haring, Virginia
  Rasmussen
1 mi. east of Calamus on Hwy. 30
319/246-2353

Camanche, Iowa

Bob Dahl's Antiques
Furniture, lamps, jewelry
1421 Washington Blvd. S. 52730
319/243-1229
By appointment only

Hansens' Antiques
A.F. Hansen
Glass, lamps, clocks, specializes in
  furniture
Hwy. 67 South 52730
319/259-5673
Open daily 12 to 5

Millstone Antiques and Things
Jane and Ken Shaw
General line antiques
820 Third St. 52730
319/259-1518; 259-8070

Charles City, Iowa

Hobert's Antiques
China, glass, lamps, furniture
603 N. Illinois St., 50616
515/288-3019
By chance or appointment

Cherokee, Iowa

G & K Antiques
510 N. 9th St. 51012
712/225-5280

Clinton, Iowa

Bob Dahl's Antiques
Furniture, lamps, jewelry
501 5th Ave. N. 52732
319/243-1229
By appointment only

Colfax, Iowa

Top of the Hill Antiques
Mary and Don Yohe
428 E. Howard 50054
South on I-80 by the water tower
515/674-3138
By chance or appointment

Corydon, Iowa

Antiques And
Maxine Jones
208 S. Franklin 50060
515/872-1469; 872-1012

Red Barn Antiques
Northeast corner of square, 50060
515/872-2075

Council Bluffs, Iowa

The Country Shop
Merle and M.J. Hayes
Primitives, wooden ware, pine
 furniture
Rt. 2, Council Bluffs 51501
9 mi. east of Council Bluffs on Hwy.
 92 to L55, ½ mi. south
712/487-3460

Lewis Township Antiques
Jim Neilsen
1400 E. South Omaha Bridge Rd.
 51501
At Neilsen Nursery, south city limits,
 just east of I-29
712/366-0551

Denison, Iowa

Olson's Antiques
Above the bakery, 51442
712/263-4241; 263-2668

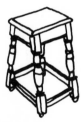

J & R House of Antiques
Bev Worley
"Antiques of all kinds"
1317 E. 23rd
515/266-4145

Leslie Reincke, Sr.
Rt. 2 from Schleswig, 2 mi. east,
 1 mi. south 51442

The Cottage Antiques
1313 Lyon St. 50316

McCarthy's Antiques
420 College Ave. 50312
515/243-1081

Woodside Antiques
Mary Fleischacker, Marcia Campbell
Primitives, collectors' items, glass,
 china, furniture
230 N.E. 66th Ave. 50313
North on U.S. 69 to first intersection
 north on Wickes Lumber, then 1
 mi. west
515/289-1212; 964-0413

Dubuque, Iowa

The Prince of Prussia
Antiques, decorations, gifts
P.O. Box 27, 491 Fourth St. W.,
 52001
319/556-8449

Eldon, Iowa

Gothic Trail Antiques
Main St., P.O. Box 12, 52554
515/652-7600

Elkader, Iowa

Red Parrot Antiques
Mrs. Virginia Wolf
716 Davidson St., N.W. 52043
319/245-2261
Open 10 to 5 except closed Tues.

Fayette, Iowa

Toutsch's House of Antiques
Evelyn and Robert Toutsch
208 E. Water St. 52142
6 blocks east of junction of 150
 and 93
319/425-3226

Fort Dodge, Iowa

Vi's Antiques
316 N. 7th St. 50501

Fredericksburg, Iowa

Blanche Sostak
"Antiques, junk and miscellaneous"
515/237-6138

Goldfield, Iowa

Field Antiques
Complete line of antiques
2 mi. north of Goldfield, 1 mi. east
  of Hwy. 17 50542
515/825-3655

Greene, Iowa

McSpaden Antiques
Assortment of antiques
129 S. Main St. 50636
1 block south of Catholic church

Violet Gift Shop
1 block south of Catholic church
  50636

Hedrick, Iowa

Hitching Post Antiques
Main St. 52563
515/653-4930

White Shutters Antiques
Main St._52563

Hinton, Iowa

Frank's Folly
10 mi. north of Sioux City, 51024
712/947-4091

Iowa City, Iowa

Judy's Iowa City Antiques
Furniture, primitives, quilts
710 S. Riverside (at Benton St.)
  52240
Located at the junction of Rts. 1, 6
  and 218
319/351-9626

Iowa City Antique Co.
Bill and Donna Launspach
20 S. Van Buren 52240
319/351-6061; 338-3717

Local Road Antiques
R.R. 5, P.O. Box 160 52240
319/351-5265

The Wine Barrel Antiques
606 S. Capitol St. 52240
319/351-6061; 338-3717

Kalona, Iowa

HalBea Antiques
Hal and Bea Moore
Primitives, furniture, collectibles,
  pottery
P.O. Box 411, 833 3rd Pl. 52247
319/656-2542

Kalona, Iowa

The Woodin Wheel
Marilyn Woodin
General line of antiques
314 B St. 52247
319/656-2240

Kensett, Iowa

Bee-Ive Antiques
General line and furniture
Main Street
Open daily except Mon.

Smalltown Antiques
Antiques, furniture stripping
Main Street
515/845-2216
By chance or appointment

LaPorte City, Iowa

The Lantern Antiques
American and European antiques,
  furniture, primitives, glass
300 Main St. 50651
12 mi. soutn of Waterloo on Hwy. 218
319/342-2024
Closed Sun. and Mon.

Lehigh, Iowa

Swanson's Farm House Antiques
John and Maggie Swanson
Furniture, primitives, collectors'
  items, china and glass
2 mi. east, 1 mi. south of Lehigh
  50557
515/359-2358

Leon, Iowa

Spicer's Antiques
102 S. White St._50144

Lester, Iowa

The Whistle Stop Antiques
Betty and Jake Kumba
General line of antiques
P.O. Box 66 51242
In the old brick depot at Lester
712/478-4433; 472-2068

Linn Grove, Iowa

Jensen's Junk-Tion
6 mi. south of town, 51033
712/296-4482

Manly, Iowa

House of Tyrrell
Furniture
123 Harris St.
515/454-2757
By chance or appointment

Maquoketa, Iowa

Banowetz Antiques
Virl Banowetz
Furniture, glassware, lamps, etc.
R.R. 1 52060
1 mi. north of Hwy. Jct. 61 and 64
  (35 mi. north of I-80)
319/652-2359

Quality Antiques
Early American country furniture,
  coverlets, pine and walnut pieces,
  refinished or rough
315 S. Niagara 52060
319/652-5370
Open Sat. & Sun., other times
  call ahead

Manson, Iowa

Elmer V. Murphy
Antiques and collectibles
1251 Main St. 50563
712/469-3706

Marion, Iowa

Original Antique Shop
933 8th Ave. 52302

Antiques by the Bullards
260 7th Ave. 52302
319/377-6007

Marshalltown, Iowa

Antique & Union Shop
106 W. Main St. 50158
515/752-0600

Bill Egleston
509A Brentwood Rd. 50158

Gene Harris Antique Center
Antique auction service
203 S. 18th Ave. 50158
Box 294
515/752-0600

Mason City, Iowa

Cobweb Corners Antiques
Furniture, glassware, primitives
915 N. Federal—Hwy. 65
515/423-2160
Open afternoons

D & S Antiques
Furniture, glassware, primitives,
children's items
515/424-2251
By appointment

Holland's Antiques
General line
Hwy. 65 North 50401
515/423-4782
By chance or appointment

Morris Sales and Auction Service
Furniture and primitives
216 S. Federal
515/324-9865
Open 12 to 5, mornings by
appointment

Treasure Chest Antiques
General line antiques
Hwy. 18 West
515/424-9005
Open afternoons and weekends
Summer: antique fairs every other
weekend

Willow Creek Antiques
Furniture, general line of quality
antiques
644 E. State St.
515/424-5568
Open most days May 1 to Dec. 1
Also by chance or appointment

Wishing Well Antiques
General line and collectibles
610 6th St., S.E.
515/423-5595
Mon.-Fri. 9 to 4 or by chance

Missouri Valley, Iowa

Hide-a-way Antiques
Max and Sara Thomas
General line furniture
Rt. 3, Box 163, 51555
712/642-2041
By chance or appointment

Mondamin, Iowa

Country Store Antiques
Larry Stevens
Specializing in oak, walnut, pine
  furniture
51557
712/646-2268
By chance or appointment

Newton, Iowa

Antiques & Collectibles
Frosty and Fran Smith
214 1st Ave. W. 50208
515/792-6891; 792-2163

Damman's Antiques
Cut glass, china, depression glass,
  furniture, picture frames, pressed
  glass
1420 1st St. N. 50208
515/792-5235

Freese Antiques
609 E. 16th St. N.   50208
515/792-9601

Charlotte Spencer
"Choice authentic antiques"
1402 N. 4th Ave. W. 50208
515/792-1669

Ocheyedan, Iowa

Timmons Antiques
51354
712/758-3126

Ogden, Iowa

The Lion's Den Antiques
Betty and Ted Swanson
General line antiques
5 mi. south on Hwy. 169 50212
515/275-4011

Osceola, Iowa

Patsy Nelson's Antiques
Antiques and collector's items
4 mi. south of Osceola, Hwy. 34
  50213
515/342-3594

Oskaloosa, Iowa

E's Hen House Antiques
Maxine Gray
Rt. 1 52577
515/672-2922

Pastanpresent Paraphernalia
Ralph and Alberta Casey
Antiques and gifts
915 High Ave. W. 52577
515/672-2759

Ottumwa, Iowa

Busy Body Antiques
Ruth W. Dotterer
General line glass, primitives,
  walnut, pine, oak furniture
309 E. Fifth St. 52501
515/682-7991

Parkersburg, Iowa

The Victorian House
50665
319/346-2511

Pella, Iowa

Huyser House
301 E. Washington St. 50219
515/628-2814

R S Pella Antiques
David Riglin, Jim Schulze
Specializir.g in furniture, general
  line
50219
515/628-1442; 628-2868
Evenings and weekends, by chance
  or appointment

Rockford, Iowa

Phelps Antiques
"Two buildings of good antiques"
123 West Main
515/756-3634
Open Tues.-Sun., also by
  appointment

Sabula, Iowa

Island City Antiques
509 Pearl St. 52070
319/687-2291

Sac City, Iowa

Freese Antiques
Southwest of courthouse, 50583

Sheffield, Iowa

Unique Antique Boutique
Furniture, primitives, lamps, clocks
Hwy. 65
515/892-8642
Mon. to Sat. 10-5

Sioux City, Iowa

Collectors' Gallery
817 W. 7th 51103
712/258-1293; 276-8078; 239-3782

Stacyville, Iowa

The Treasure Hut
Marian Pitzen
Antiques, furniture, orientals,
  collectibles, glassware, primitives
Main St. 50476
515/737-2598
Tues.-Sat. 10 to 5
Sun. & Mon. by chance or
  appointment

Sumner, Iowa

Heavenly Daze Antiques
122 E. Main 50674

Swisher, Iowa

Peterka's Antiques & Cane Shop
John and Lil Peterka
Specialists in chair seats and hand-
  crafted doll furniture
R.R. 1 52338
319/857-3072
By chance or appointment

Swisher, Iowa

The Wood Shed
Gary and Patty Seger, Pat
  Beardsley
Antique furniture, primitives, gifts,
  refinishing
Summit Ave. & 2nd St. 52338
319/857-2915

Tripoli, Iowa

Main Street Antiques
The Kruegers
General line antiques
301 S. Main St. 50676
Thurs. 6 to 9 p.m.
Sat., Sun. 10 to 5 and by
  appointment

Wapello, Iowa

'Tiques 'N Things
Downtown, 52653
319/523-8230

Washburn, Iowa

Gene Waltemeyer
7059 LaPorte Rd. 50706
319/296-2149

Waterloo, Iowa

Candle Glow Antiques
Refinished furniture, decorative
  accent pieces
255 Derbyshire 50701
Weekday afternoons except Thurs.,
  or by appointment

Pilot House Antiques
266 Falls Ave. 50701
319/232-5414

Webster City, Iowa

Dorothy Brim
Furniture, collectibles, clocks
Rt. 3 50595
5 mi. north and 4½ mi. east of
  Webster City
By chance or appointment

Hargrave's Antiques
Ivan and Ann Hargrave
Hwy. 20 West 50595
515/832-4070

Wellman, Iowa

Bloom Antiques and Collectibles
Rex and Phyllis Bloom
52356
319/646-2650; 646-2887
Open daily 9 to 5:30, Sun. by
  appointment

West Union, Iowa

Old Mill
Antique shop and bottle museum
Hwy. 18 East
319/422-5283

Michigan

Northern Michigan, like northern Wisconsin and northern Minnesota, comes alive in the summer, so check shop hours in that area carefully. The Grand Rapids Public Museum, with its displays of Grand Rapids-made furniture, is open on weekdays from 10 to 5 and on Sunday afternoons. The Henry Ford Museum at Dearborn houses one of the best collections in the country of furniture, ceramics, glass, pewter, silver, and textiles dating back to the Pilgrim period. Romeo, north of Detroit and southeast of Flint, is a historic district with fine old 19th century homes and several antique shops.

Adrian, Michigan

The Shopkeeper
Mary and George Von Wahlde
General line antiques, 7,000 sq. ft.,
  mainly furniture and decorative
  accessories
325 E. Maumee St. 49221
Tues.-Thurs., Sat. 11 to 5:30
Fri. 11 to 9; Closed Mon., Sun.,
  except holiday season

Allegan, Michigan

Worden's Antiques
B.A. Worden
General line antiques, furniture,
  clocks
505 Grand St. 49010
616/673-6585
7 days, by chance or appointment

Ann Arbor, Michigan

Old Brick Antiques
American antiques, many refinished,
  large stock
512 S. Main
313/761-0696
Mon.-Sat. 10 to 5

Battle Creek, Michigan

Dempsey's Antiques
Wholesale/retail
1423 E. Michigan Ave. on Bus. I-94
  49017
616/964-7466

The Lost & Found Shop
Gloria Murray
549 Capital Ave., S.W. 49015
616/964-4048; 963-9284
Open Tues.-Sat. 10 to 5

Bay City, Michigan

Yesteryear Shop
Howard H. and Arlene Herzberger,
  Howard and Pamela Herzberger
General line antiques, furniture,
  glassware, primitives, curios
Free coffee and antique conversation
1203 Columbus Ave. 48706
517/892-2394; evenings 892-1358 or
  895-5974
Mon.-Fri. 8 to 5; Sat. 8 to noon;
  evenings by appointment

Bellaire, Michigan

Ports of Call
Furniture and china
Sat. only, 10:30 to 5, May to Oct.

Bellevue, Michigan

Lewis What-Not Shop
Antiques and dolls
2 mi. east on Battle Creek Hwy.,
RFD 2, Box 60
616/763-9972
Mon.-Fri. 9 to 5

Big Rapids, Michigan

W & D Antiques
Furniture, collectibles
10545 Northland Dr.
616/796-5181; 796-5119

Brighton, Michigan

The Dunks' Puritan Farms
Madge Dunk
Victorian furniture, antique prints,
  decorator items, collectibles
3400 Pleasant Valley Rd. 48116
313/229-4516
Thurs.-Sun. 10 to 5

Hope Lake Store
Betty Hatfield
Antiques, collectibles, coins,
  sterling flatware
3225 US 23 48116
313/227-7614
Thurs.-Sun. 12:30 to 5

Byron, Michigan

Greek Revival House Antiques
"137-year-old house filled with
  quality antiques and collectibles"
11355 Rolston Rd. (20 min. from
  Flint)
313/266-4850
Sat. & Sun. 11 to 6 or by
  appointment

Carleton, Michigan

Pat's Antiques
Furniture, primitives, art glass,
  miscellaneous
14017 Carleton West Rd. 48117
  (8 mi. west of State Police Post at
  Flat Rock on Will Carleton Dr.,
  south on Carleton West Rd. to
  second on right side)
313/654-6668
7 days, 12 to 5

Charlotte, Michigan

Newman's Antiques
Jerry and Val Newman
General line antiques, furniture, art,
  glass, cut glass
730 W. Lawrence 48813
517/543-3216
By chance or appointment

Clinton, Michigan

Scott's Antiques
Mildred Scott
General line antiques, primitives,
  Victorian furniture, china, glass,
  Oriental items
202 Division Ave.
313/456-4460
May to Nov.: Mon.-Fri. 9 to 5 or by
  appointment

Coldwater, Michigan

Abbott's Antiques
Primitives, tin, glass and furniture
315 Fiske Rd. 40936 (½ mi. east of
  I-69 on US 12, turn right ½ mi.)
517/278-6729
Closed Thurs. and Fri.; other days
  9 to 5

Maples Antiques
Mr. and Mrs. John J. Capella
General line antiques
441 E. Chicago St. 49036
517/278-2294
April thru Nov.: Mon.-Sun. 9 to 6

Wolfe's Antique Shop
Daisy Wolf
General line antiques
22 Morse St. 40936
517/278-6980
Mon.-Sun. 8 to 4

Coloma, Michigan

Paw Paw Lake Antiques
Vernette Lewis
General line antiques
Paw Paw Lake Rd. and Lakewood
  Dr. 49038
616/468-6452
April thru Aug.: Mon.-Sun. 9 to 5
Labor Day thru April-by appoint-
  ment or chance

Detroit, Michigan

A-1 Good Used Furniture
Bob Mazzola
Furniture, lamps, glass, dishes,
  silverware. Antique appraiser,
  specializing in curved glass china
  cabinets and antique desks
13906 Mack
313/823-4888

Antique Village
Angie Dean
Antiques and restaurant — general
  line, primitives, gifts
16000 E. Warren
313/TU 5-1655; PR 9-9259
Mon.-Fri. 4 p.m. to 4 a.m.

Century House Antiques
Furniture, brass beds, glass, jewelry,
  silver, lamps, books, coins,
  collector's items
20110 W. McNichols
313/835-8080

Schmidt's Antique Shop
  (see Ypsilanti)

Town and Country Antiques
Furniture, brass beds, lamps, glass,
  jewelry, dolls
19835 W. McNichols Rd.
313/358-1298; 358-4474

Eaton Rapids, Michigan

Silhouette Antique Shop
Dorothy Hemans
General line antiques, dolls, art
  glass
315 S. Main St. 48827
517/663-4777
Tues.-Sat. 10 to 5; Sun. 2 to 5

Fenton, Michigan

Mill Site Antiques
Mary Litteral
General line antiques, primitives,
  wooden ware, pottery, glass, china,
  furniture
Located in small village with grist-
  mill stream
6045 S. Linden 48430
313/629-4560
Thurs.-Sun. 11 to 5

Silver Star Antiques
Mrs. Florence Kardoe
Imported and American antiques,
  specializing in Victorian and carved
  furniture, lamps, clocks, glass,
  china, brass, copper, pewter,
  ironware
5900 Green Rd., Rt. 3 49430
  (between Brighton and Fenton, use
  Clude Rd. exit west 3 mi. then north
  ¾ mi. on Green Rd.)
517/546-0686
Mon. thru Sat. 9 to 6

Flat Rock, Michigan

*Yesterday Shop (M. White's
  Antiques)*
Antiques, handmade items
26161 E. Huron River Dr. 48134
313/782-1740
Tues.-Sat. 10 to 5; Sun. 12 to 5

Freesoil, Michigan

Andy's Antiques
Harry T. Anderson
Antiques and collectibles in an old
  barn
Rt. 1, US 31
616/757-3569
May - Oct., 7 days a week, 8 a.m.
  to dark

Fremont, Michigan

Mae's Antiques
Mae Norton
General line antiques, no
  reproductions
5445 Green Ave. 49412
616/924-2273
All year, by chance or appointment

Glen Arbor, Michigan

Weathervane Antiques
Robert and Iole Kelly
Decorative accessories, curios
6391 Western Ave., M-22, 49636
616/334-3760
June thru Sept., Mon. thru Sun. 10
  to 5

Goodrich, Michigan

Gray's Top-A-Wingo Antiques
Dennis Gray
General line antiques
8168 S. State
313/636-2422
Sat., Sun. 11 to 5

Grand Ledge, Michigan

The Sign of the Peacock
Quality antiques: furniture, glass,
  pottery, jewelry, primitives,
  porcelain
202 S. Bridge St.   48837
517/627-7722
Mon.-Sat. 10 to 5

Hastings, Michigan

Barlow Gardens Flowers
Norman Barlow
Antiques, wholesale and retail,
  retail florist
1505 S. Jefferson   49058
616/945-5029; 945-2132
Mon.-Sat. 8 to 5

Yankee Trader Antiques
Betty Hammond
Antiques, collector's items, arts,
  crafts, appraisals
233 S. Michigan   49058
616/945-9691
Tues.-Sun. 10 to 6; Sun. 10 to 4 or
  by appointment

Highland Park, Michigan

B.C. Antiques
Cleon Chase
American country furniture and
  accessories
16543 Hamilton, 48203
313/862-7197
Mon.-Sat. 10 to 5

Bess Orman Antiques
Bess Orman
Glass, china, furniture
16559 Hamilton, 48203
313/861-2878
Mon.-Sat. 11 to 5:30

The Dandelion Shop
Mrs. Earl Frost
Furniture, glass, china, collectibles
16400 Hamilton, 48203
Tues.-Thurs., Sat. 12 to 4:30

The Golden Pallette
General line antiques, furniture,
  repairs and refinishing
16621 Hamilton, 48203
313/345-8669
Mon.-Sat. 10 to 5

John Bryant Antiques
John Bullock
Primitives, glass, chandeliers,
  refinished furniture, prints, frames
16517 Hamilton, 48203
313/368-2726
Mon.-Sat. 12 to 5

Leonard Berry Antiques
Leonard Berry
American furniture, custom lamps
16527 Hamilton 48203
313/864-5584
Mon.-Sat. 11 to 5

Merwin's Antiques
Ronald Winter
General line antiques
16810 Hamilton 48203
Mon.-Sat. 10 to 5

The Push Cart Antiques
Florence Cox
General line antiques
16806 Hamilton 48203
313/891-3927
Mon.-Sat. 10 to 6

Nelson Therrien Antiques
Nelson Therrien
American country furniture, handmade light fixtures
16513 Hamilton 48203
313/864-9040
Mon.-Sat. 11 to 5

Sign of the Red Squirrel
Jean Van Dyke
Victorian furniture, clocks
16539 Hamilton 48203
313/341-9466
Wed.-Sat. 12 to

Hubbard Lake, Michigan

The Cedar Trunk
Ronald L. and Sharon L. Smith
General line antiques, primitives,
  furniture, glass. Specializing in bird
  carvings, antiques, and arts and
  crafts of the area
Box 16 B
517/727-2877
Memorial Day to Labor Day, 7 days,
  9 to 6

Ironwood, Michigan

Kornwolf's Antiques
Furniture, lamps, primitives
P.O. Box 581 49938
906/932-3124

Iron Mountain, Michigan

The Cobweb Antiques
Richard Williams
Antique brass beds, furniture,
  china, glass, primitives, copper,
  brass, clocks, jewelry, pictures
North US 2 49081
906/774-6560
Mon.-Thurs., Sat. 9 to 5; Fri. 9 to 9

Nora K. Shop Antiques
Norman J. and Nora K. Flemington
General line antiques
837 E. "B" St. 49801
906/774-4545
7 days, 9 to 5

The Wishing Well
Donald Khoury
General line antiques and collectibles
203 E. "A" St. 49801
906/774-7700
Mon.-Thurs., Sat. 9 to 5; Fri. 9 to 9

Antique Cottage
Primo and Ethel Turvessi
Furniture, primitives, clocks, lamps,
cut glass, stained glass, dishes
Ice Road
906/CO 5-9753
May thru Oct. 7 days, 8 to 5

Banzhaf's
Karl Banshaf (winter: 2111 Arling-
ton Ave., Middleton, Ohio)
Furniture, primitives, brass, copper,
china, glass, lamps, dolls,
postcards, pictures, frames, musical
items, books
Sprawling shop of 5 buildings
8 mi. west of Iron River; 6 mi. due
west on US 2, then 2 mi. south
on 436
June 20 thru early Sept. Wed.,
Thurs. *only*, 9:30 to 5:30

Jackson, Michigan

Mary Middlebrook
General line antiques
7516 E. Michigan Ave. 49201
517/764-3635
7 days, by chance or appointment

Jonesville, Michigan

Souveniers of Yesteryear
William Gamble
Fine Victorian furniture, china,
glassware, American antiques
dating from 1840 to 1900
211 Maumee 49250
517/849-9153
7 days, by chance or appointment

Kalamazoo, Michigan

Heritage House Antiques
Don Wagner
General line antiques, American
antiques, guns, reproduction
hardware
2815 Lake St. 49001
616/349-6156
Tues.-Sun. 1 to 5

Kalkaska, Michigan

Old Mill Antiques
Ruth Primer
General line antiques, primitives,
furniture, glassware, china,
jewelry, books
Located in 96-year-old building
616/258-9461
April thru Oct. Mon.-Sat. 9 to 6;
Sun. 7 to 6

Kingston, Michigan

Barron's Antiques
Robert Barron
General line antiques
5969 State St.
313/683-2750
Mon.-Sat. 10 to 6

Lake Leelanau, Michigan

Nautic Antiques
Old furniture, artifacts, lamps,
primitives
Daily except Thursday, 10 to 5, May
to October

Lake Orion, Michigan

Remember When
Carol Korn
Antiques and collectibles
2355 Joslyn Ct. 48035
313/391-2311
Tues.-Sat. 10 to 5; Sun. 12 to 5

Y Knot Antiques
Betty Miller
Miscellaneous, parts and supplies
 for old lamps
2325 Joslyn Ct. 48035
313/391-3033
Tues.-Sat. 10 to 5; Sun. 11 to 5

Lakeside, Michigan

Heritage House Antiques
General line antiques
Red Arrow Hwy. 49116
Mon.-Fri. 12 to 6 (except Jan.-
 March, by appointment)

Lapeer, Michigan

Peppermill Antiques
M. L. Stanfill
General line antiques, specializing in
 clocks and furniture, antique clock
 repair
2108 Peppermill Rd. 48446
313/664-9848
Summer: 10 to 6; Winter: 10 to 5

Leonidas, Michigan

Century Store Antiques
Robert and Marian Mayer
Furniture, primitives, glassware (2
 buildings)
M 60 and M 66
616/496-7535
Mon.-Sat. 1 to 5 except closed Thurs.
 in winter. Mornings by appointment

Lowell, Michigan

Country Schoolhouse
General line antiques
52 St. at Bancroft
517/868-5421
April thru Dec. by chance or
 appointment (check at house)

Ludington, Michigan

Fruit Cellar Antiques
General line, featuring primitives,
 glassware, furniture, collectibles
Rt. 1, Olmstead Rd. 49134
616/843-3618
10 to 10 by chance or appointment

Karen Allen Antiques
Small furniture, glassware
Chair covering lessons and supplies
Rt. 3, Stiles Rd. 49134
616/843-8701
Summer: 7 days 10 to 6; Winter:
 Mon.-Fri. by appointment or
 chance

Luther, Michigan

Hopeful Antiques
Gordon L. and Ruth E. Marks
Antiques and collectibles—money-
back guarantee, no reproductions
Pine River
616/829-3977
July and Aug. 7 days, 9 to 9

Mackinaw City, Michigan

Antique Valley
Pat Barnett
General line antiques
219 Central Ave.
616/436-5246
June to mid-Sept. 7 days,
10 to 5

Marshall, Michigan

J and J Antiques
Joyce Tolan
General line antiques, clocks,
furniture, dishes, dolls
18025 Division Dr. 49068
616/781-5581
Mon.-Fri 10 to 5

Strong's Antiques
General line, specializing in refinished furniture ("All antiques are
from the attic")
227 E. Michigan Ave. 49068
616/781-5260
Tues.-Sat. 9 to 5; Sun. 2 to 5

Ye Olde Pump House Antiques
Agnes Heath
Furniture, lamps, pressed glass,
dolls, art glass, iron, post cards,
pictures, trunks
US 27, 49068 (6 mi. south of
Marshall, then 1 mi. east on H
Drive South)
Farm setting, tame deer
616/781-8728
By chance

McBain, Michigan

Grandmother's Barn
Bernease Pelty
General line antiques
Hwy . 66, 49657
616/825-2203
Seasonal—call for schedule

Mears, Michigan

Muriel's Antiques
General line antiques, furniture,
primitives, china, glass
Silver Lake 49436
616/873-3076
7 days, 10 to 6

Monroe, Michigan

Meyer's Antiques
Calvin Meyers
American general line antiques,
primitives, specializing in American
and foreign clocks and repairs
1184 S. Raisinville Rd. 48161
Mon.-Fri.; in evenings by
appointment

Muskegon, Michigan

The Antique Shop
General line antiques
1342 Peck St.
616/722-3281
Mon.-Sat. 9 to 5

New Buffalo, Michigan

Rainbow's End
General line antiques and art objects
Rt. 1, Box 572 49117
616/756-9291
June thru Sept.: Mon.-Fri. 10 to 6
Oct. thru May: weekends only, 10 to 6

Niles, Michigan

Lois Antiques and Such
Dishes, clocks, furniture,
  miscellaneous
1008 Oak St. 49120
616/683-7224
Tues. thru Sat. 10 to 5

Clevering Antiques
General line antiques, china, glass,
  clocks, jewelry
36 South Fifth 49120
616/683-3647
Mon.-Sun. noon to 6 or by
  appointment

Otsego, Michigan

Lanz Antiques
Zeda Lanz
Art glass, lamps, clocks, china,
  collectibles
377 W. Morrell St. 49078
616/694-2847
Mon.-Fri. 8 to 5

Oxford, Michigan

Parisi Antiques
Mrs. Victoria Parisi
Furniture, copper, brass, art glass,
  iron fencing, gates, lighting fixtures,
  primitives
796 Rochester Rd.
313/752-3437
7 days, 11 to 5:30; evenings by
  appointment

Plainwell, Michigan

Barber's Antiques
Mabel Barber
Antiques, fine china, glass,
  miscellaneous
All merchandise guaranteed
418 Park St.,
616/685-5562
By chance or appointment

The Rain Barrel Antiques
Victorian furniture, primitives,
  dishes, glassware
Quaint shop in rustic surroundings
675 N. 10th St. (1½ mi. north of old
  US 131)
616/685-8652
Year round

Pontiac, Michigan

Shoppe of Antiquity
Primitives, furniture, wooden ware,
 china, glassware
Small antique tool museum
7766 Highland Rd. 48054
313/673-0301
Tues.-Sun. 10 to 5

Potterville, Michigan

Elegante Junque & Antiques
Ellie Wysack, Jan Hunsberger
Furniture, primitives, clocks, dolls,
 glassware, toys, banks, collectibles
On US 27 (Temporary 169)
517/543-1631; 645-7325; 627-3106
Sat. and Sun. 10 to 7 (a flea market)

Quincy, Michigan

Wentworth's Antiques
Doran and Virginia Wentworth
General line antiques
In the heart of the lake region
11 E. Jefferson St.
517/639-9525
Weekends and evenings only
 (call ahead)

Rapid City, Michigan

Stuart and Isabella Miller's
Antiques and primitives

Reading, Michigan

Ye Olde Yoke Antiques
Robert Oswald
General line antiques
119 E. Silver St. 49274
517/283-2763
By chance or appointment

Romeo, Michigan

The Bayberry House
Mr. and Mrs. Robert Bartig
General line antiques, specializing
 in primitives
264 N. Main St. 48065
Shop is in one of Romeo's historic
 homes, a board and batten Gothic
 Victorian, c. 1849
313/752-9789
Tues.-Sat. 11 to 5

Charlotte Henry Antiques
Antique furniture and fine glass,
 china, lamps
222 N. Main 48065
313/752-7055
Mon.-Sat. 10 to 5

*Edward Jones Floorcovering and
 Antiques*
Jane Jones
American primitives, handhooked
 rugs, books published by Romeo
Historical Society ("Romeo is a
 state and federal historic district, a
 19th century village")
229 N. Main 48065
313/752-9925
Tues.-Sat. 10 to 5

Romeo, Michigan

My Friend and I Shop
Chloan Smith and Marilyn Foltz
General line antiques
"Quaint shop in historical town with
  pleasant old homes and tree-lined
  streets"
224 N. Main 48065
7 days, 9 to 5

Saginaw, Michigan

Heritage Antiques
Furniture, glassware, primitives,
  jewelry. Appraisals, estate service
2375 S. Thomas Rd.
517/792-9146
Mon.-Sat. 11 to 5; Sun. by
  appointment only

Saugatuck, Michigan

Main Street Antiques
Frank Van Antelek
Furniture, primitives, jewelry, china,
  glass, collectibles
119 Butler St. 49453
616/857-5351
April thru Dec., Mon.-Sat. 10:30 to
  5:30; Sun. 12 to 5

Scottsville, Michigan

Centennial Antique Farm
Brass beds, furniture
Stiles Rd., Rt. 2
616/845-5902
7 days, 10 to 6

Sebewaing, Michigan

Bill's Antiques
Bill Fournien
General line antiques, primitives
M 25
313/883-3190
Summer: by chance or appointment

Standish, Michigan

Bissonnette's House of Antiques
Victor and Pauline Bissonette
Refinished furniture, clocks, lamps,
  dolls, glassware, no reproductions
Clocks finished and repaired
Rt. 2, Box 296 48658
7 days 9 to 5; by appointment to 9
  (best to call ahead)

St. Clair, Michigan

Betty Lou Dushane, Antiques
General line antiques
302 Thornapple St. 48079
313/329-4442
7 days, 12 to 5

Taylor, Michigan

Shuttle Shop
General line antiques, clocks,
  furniture, glass, clock parts
8810 S. Telegraph
Mon,-Sat. 11 to 5

Temperance, Michigan

Stark's Antiques
Mrs. Stark
General line antiques
4532 M 151 (2 mi. east of express-
way 23)
313/856-1148
Mon.-Fri. 8 to 5

Three Oaks, Michigan

Heirloom House Antiques
Antiques and gifts: furniture, dishes,
glassware, miscellaneous
207 Sycamore St.
616/756-9821
April thru Dec. 7 days, 9 to 5 or
by appointment

Traverse City, Michigan

Gull Gallery
John Moore
Antiques, paintings, clocks,
furniture, prints, pottery, gifts
Conducted tours
3717 Jefferson Rd.
616/947-4158
April thru Sept., Mon.-Sun. 10 to 7
(Winter: call first)

This Old Barn
Susan Feiger
Antiques and collectibles: furniture,
glassware, farm tools, bottles,
jewelry, quilts, postcards
2513 Nelson Rd. (7 mi. north of
Traverse City on Old Mission
Peninsula; take M 37 to first road
past Kroupa's Factory, turn west)
616/223-4833
March thru Dec. 7 days, 10 to 6 or
by appointment

Troy, Michigan

Apple Tree in Troy
Alice Kopke and Donna Hall
General line antiques, books, quilts
and coverlets
Early American folk art lessons
65 E. Square Lake Rd. 48054
313/879-1674
Tues.-Sat. 12 to 4:30; Sun. 1 to 5

Jinny's Antiques
General line antiques, furniture,
china, collectibles
59 E. Square Lake Rd. 48084
313/879-0116
Tues.-Sat. 12 to 4:30; Sun. 1:30 to 5

Union City, Michigan

Plantation Antiques
Mrs. Neal Radebaugh
General line antiques specializing in
glassware, china, buttons, quilts
handmade laces, lamps, toys,
books, some furniture
In 1861 home with 20 rooms,
landscaped grounds
Rt. 2, Box 218 49094
517/741-8023
By appointment only

Warren, Michigan

Country Fair Flea Market
Chuck Holland
Antiques, collectibles, crafts,
  auctions, farm market
13899 8-Mile Rd. (just east of
  Schoenherr)
313/779-3070
Sat. & Sun. 9 to 6

Watervliet, Michigan

Nordhoff's Antiques
Larry and Liz Nordhoff
General line antiques, jewelry,
  stamps, coins. Stripping, refinishing,
  recaning, reupholstering of antiques
248 Huntoon Ave. 49098
Rt. 3, Box 277
616/463-6050
By appointment only

West Branch, Michigan

The Country House
Loraine Bell
General line antiques, collectibles
1349 Dow Rd.
517/345-0831
April thru Nov. 7 days, 9 to 6

Whitehall, Michigan

The Pack Rats
Cal and Katey Halberg
General line of antiques and collectibles including furniture, no
  reproductions, 14 rooms
Serious collectors and dealers
  invited
116 W. Slocum 49461
616/893-6885
Tues.-Sun. 10 to 6

White Cloud, Michigan

R & E Variety
Rosetta Green
Furniture, dishes, miscellaneous,
  depression glass
Rt. 4 M 37
616/689-2036
7 days, 9 to 6, evenings by
  appointment

Ypsilanti, Michigan

Schmidt's Antique Shop
Furniture and collector's items,
  many imported. Unrestricted
  auctions the first Saturday and pre-
  ceding Friday of each month
Retail sales daily 9 to 5 except
  Sunday, 11 to 5
5138 W. Michigan Ave. 48147
313/434-2660

❀ **Minnesota** ❀

Three areas rich in antiques in Minnesota are Hiawatha Valley (Zumbro Falls, Lake City, Red Wing, Welch, Etter, Cottage Grove) in the southeastern part of the state; Wenonah-land (La Crescent, Dakota, Mabel, Winona, Houston, Fountain City, Centerville, Galesville, Wisconsin) in the southeastern corner; and Detroit Lakes in midstate, east of Fargo and west of Duluth. Many northern Minnesota shops have seasonal schedules, so check before planning a visit. Watch for examples of country furniture made by Northern European craftsmen.

Albert Lea, Minnesota

The Heart of the Artichoke
General line, collector's items, handcrafts
222 E. Clark (downtown)
Weekdays 10 to 5
From 1 to 5 first Sun. each month June-Sept.

Austin, Minnesota

Len's Antiques
Leonard Smisek, Jr.
Specializing in furniture
616 7th St. N.E. 55912
507/433-9901; 433-5272
Tues.-Sat. 12 to 5 or by appointment

Baudette, Minnesota

Riverside Antiques
Gwen Newton
Hwy. 172, 2 mi. north of Baudette 56623
218/634-2859
11 to 6 except closed most Mondays

Bloomington Prairie, Minnesota

Ebeling's Wholesale-Retail Antiques
Bruce and Hjordes Ebeling
"Huge clean stock, every category"
415 E. Main 55917
507/583-2093; 583-2904
Mon.-Sat. 9 to 5 or by appointment

Butterfield, Minnesota

The Rainbow Antiques
Al and Laura Lorenz
New and used items
56120
507/956-2646
Open Thurs. and by chance or appointment

Cottage Grove, Minnesota

Tin Cup
"Things of yesteryear"
8155 Belden Blvd.
612/459-5132
Weekdays 4 to 9; weekends 10 to 5

Crosby, Minnesota

Bits of Yesteryear
Mattie Broden
Collectibles, furniture
4 - 3rd Ave. S.W. 56441
218/546-6639, 546-5261

Dakota, Minnesota

Apple Country Antiques
Connie Kubista
General line
RFD 1
9 to 5 daily, May 1 - Oct. 31

Resale и nd Antiques
Charlotte Uehling
General line of antiques and
  collectibles
507/643-6716
Closed Fri. except by appointment

Detroit Lakes, Minnesota

Americana House
¼ mi. west of Shoreham on Lake
  Sallie
R.R. 1

Cobwebs Unlimited
5 mi. south of Detroit Lakes on
  Hwy. 59
Open until Labor Day
Flea markets during summer (check
  for dates)

Hide A Way Antiques
Roy and Harriette Lorentz
Furniture, glassware, primitives
1½ mi. past country club golf
  course, County Rd. 17
218/847-3324

Margaret's Antiques
Antiques, collector's items, reference
  books
2 mi. north on Hwy. 59
218/847-8487

Muench's
Furniture, toys, collectibles
832 Washington Ave.
218/847-8459

Tom's Antiques
1160 Washington Ave.

Dunnell, Minnesota

Roggow House Antiques
Bill and Joy Roggow
Glass, china, furniture, junk
56127
507/695-2561

Faribault, Minnesota

Stoeckel's
Antique clocks and dolls
615 N.W. 3rd St.   55021
507/334-7772
By chance or appointment

Geneva, Minnesota

Milo Craft
Antiques, collectibles, fine restored
  furniture
103 2nd St. S.E.   56035
507/256-7696

Glenville, Minnesota

Countryside Antiques
Russel Tordoff and Willis Pfieffer
Furniture, dishes, kerosene lamps,
  collector's items
56036
507/448-2855; 448-3515

Good Thunder, Minnesota

E. & L. Fitzsimmons
"Largest antique shop in area"
Full line of antiques and collectibles

Grand Rapids, Minnesota

Crystal Lake Antiques
Joyce Hein
Antiques, collectibles
1115 3rd Ave., N.W. on Hwy. 38
  North 55744
218/326-4890
By chance or appointment

Walter & Ruth Schack Antiques
General antiques, glass, clocks,
  dishes, furniture
"Area's largest stock"
605 11th Ave., N.E. 55744
218/326-3937
Open 7 days

Lamb-tiques
Furniture, glassware, collectibles
117 E. 5th
612/437-9697
Open 7 days

Hastings, Minnesota

Odd and Olds
Robert and Vi Adams
Furniture and glassware
Hwy. 316

Hibbing, Minnesota

Heritage Antiques
Victorian, depression, primitives
2801 4th Ave., W. 55746
218/263-4368
By appointment only

Houston, Minnesota

Witts Antiques
Marion J. Witt
Antiques, collector's items
RFD 2
507/896-3794
By chance or appointment

Hovland, Minnesota

Hovland Antiques
H. Drabik
55606
218/475-2359

Kasson, Minnesota

*Innkeeper's Antiques and Almost
  Antiques*
Peg and Glenn Thomson
Furniture, china, glassware, clocks
Kasson Hotel 55944
507/634-3711

Kennedy, Minnesota

Olde Tyme Shoppe
Barbara Swenson
Antiques, gifts, country store
218/674-3626

Lake City, Minnesota

Summer Kitchen
"Antiques of all kinds"
522 N. Lakeshore Dr.
612/345-2883

Lakeville, Minnesota

Fair Acres Farm
Bob and Mary Johnson
Primitives, antiques, collectibles
8684 250th St., W.   55044
612/469-2385

Mabel, Minnesota

Victoriana
Dwayne and Diana Houdek
General line plus refinished
  Victorian, walnut furniture
507/493-5696
"If we're home, we're open"

Mankato, Minnesota

Bargain Center
Ila Bergien
"Grandma's treasures" furniture,
  miscellaneous
731 S. Front St., 56001
507/338-1834

Willard's Colonial House Antiques
Hugh and Eileen Willard
Old glass, china, furniture,
  primitives
20 Skyline Dr.   56001
507/387-2400
"If we're home, we're open"

Mapleton, Minnesota

Jim Annis Antiques
Glass, china, furniture, primitives
2 mi. south, 1½ mi. west of
  Mapleton
By chance or appointment

Marine-on-the-St. Croix, Minnesota

River Valley Antiques
John M. Affolter
19097 St. Croix Trl. N.

McGregor, Minnesota

Taylor's Antiques
"Large stock of general antiques"
Big Sandy Lake at Prairie
  River Bridge
218/426-3300

Medford, Minnesota

Plantation Shop
Wilfred and Helen Kelsey
Antiques and used items of all kinds
1 mi. west of 35W on County Rd. 23
507/451-1485

Minneapolis, Minnesota

Duane's Antiques & Things, Inc.
Furniture, glassware, clocks,
  curios, primitives
1705 Arthur St. N.E.
612/780-1561
Open 12 to 6 every day except
Mon.

The Little Antique Shop
Wilbur F., Dana M. and Gary
  F. Hodge
4404 Beard Ave. S. 55410
612/823-4787
Tues.-Fri. 1 to 5:30; Sat. 10 to 6;
  Sun. 1 to 6

Monticello, Minnesota

The Red Granary
David and Lorraine Newkirk
Primitives, crockery, lamps and
  accessories, spoon rings
Rt. 3, Box 141 55362
612/295-5704
By appointment

New Ulm, Minnesota

Grandma's Garage
Hunce and Linda Hemberger
Antiques and collectibles
213 S. State St. 56073
507/359-9187
By chance

Oakland, Minnesota

His and Her Treasures
Arliss E. Davis
Antiques, collectibles, crafts
3½ mi. west of Austin on County
  Rd. 46 56706
507/437-1622
By chance or appointment

Owatonna, Minnesota

Country Antiques
Mary and Harvey Grunwald
3 mi. northeast on Mineral Springs
  Rd., then 3/10 mi. north on Kenyon
  Rd. 55060
507/451-4844

Racine, Minnesota

Patio Place
Evelyn Mayer
Antiques, glass, china, primitives
1 mi. south, 2 mi. west
507/378-2386
By chance or appointment

Red Wing, Minnesota

George Enz
Historic Graham House: Fine
  antiques and accessories
Busch House: Furniture in the rough
625 W. 5th St.
612/388-2650

Graham House Annex
Gloria, Gracie, Carol, Peggy
"Shop within a shop"
General line of antiques and
  Americana
625 W. 5th St.
612/388-2650
Open daily 11 to 5; Sun. 1 to 5

Red Wing, Minnesota

Strucks
Specializing in unusual and antique
  furniture, glassware, old bottles, etc.
Hwy. 19, R.R. 2
612/388-6875
Open 7 days

Teahouse
"Historic Octagon House"
General line of antiques
927 W. 3rd St.
612/388-3669
Open daily except Sunday

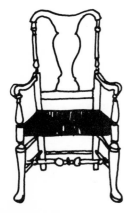

Rochester, Minnesota

Sunshine Shop
Neal Nelson
Antiques, used furnishings,
  tapestries
Center at Broadway
507/289-1969
Mon.-Sat. 10 to 5
Sun. 12 to 5

Rosemount, Minnesota

The Country Store
Mayme and Clinton Kolb
Antiques and reproductions
120 St. at Hwy. 3   55068
612/423-1242

St. Cloud, Minnesota

Early America Antiques
Patrick T. Fouquette
102 E. St. Germain   56301

St. James, Minnesota

Country Aire Antiques
Furniture, primitives, glass
4 mi. north Hwy. 4, ½ mi. west
  Hwy. 30
507/375-3869

313 Antiques
Furniture, glassware, primitives,
  collectibles
Downtown
507/375-3869
By chance or appointment

St. Paul, Minnesota

Bob's Antiques
203 Vernon St.   55105
612/699-1933

J & E Antiques
"500 pieces of furniture. One of the
  state's largest"
1000 Arcade (Hwy. 61)
612/771-9654

Spicer, Minnesota

Guy & Gladys Saulsbury Antiques
56288

Taylors Falls, Minnesota

Wooden Horse Antiques, Inc.
Furniture, glass, china, clocks.
Antique auction on fourth Sat. of
  each month, Welch Bros. auctioneer
P.O. Box 232 55084
612/465-6111

Wayzata, Minnesota

"The Way It Was" of Wayzata
Bonnie R. Bunker
Country primitives and antiques
523 E. Lake St. 55191
612/472-3616

Welch, Minnesota

Welch Village
Country antiques
County Rd. 7, P.O. Box 127
612/388-4503
Open weekends 12 to 5, weekdays
  by chance

West Red Wing, Minnesota

Fishers
Furniture and glassware
Hwy. 61
612/388-9807

Winona, Minnesota

Mary Twyce Antiques & Books
Mary Pendleton
Antiques, rare books
920 W. 5th St.
507/454-4412
10 to 5 daily except closed Sun.

Robert Mathot
Primitives, refinished furniture
122 E. 2nd St.
Open afternoons

Zumbro Falls, Minnesota

The Tin Cup
Cecil and Rachel Morris
General line of antiques and
  collectibles
Hwy. 63, P.O. Box 293
507/753-2957
Open Wed., Thurs., Sat., Sun. 11 to
  5 or by appointment

Zumbro Valley Antiques
Allen and Sharon Graves
Specializing in furniture
R.R. 1 55991
507/753-2398
Wed.-Sun. 9 to 5 or by appointment

Wisconsin

Country furniture made by local craftsmen can be found fairly frequently in Wisconsin. Keep an eye out for Scandinavian and German designs, as well as some examples of designs from other Northern European countries. Mass-produced turn-of-the-century oak and furniture from the 1920s is readily available. Visit Pioneer Village of Ozaukee County, northwest of Port Washington to see how Wisconsin settlers lived in the years 1840-1865. In Fond du Lac, the Galloway House and Village restorations exemplify the Wisconsin of Victorian times. Galloway House is a 30-room Italianate mansion that has been restored by the Fond du Lac County Historical Society.

Abbotsford, Wisconsin

Town House
Dorothy Mazza
123 N. Hwy. 13 54405
Farm House
2 mi. north on Hwy. 13 and 1 mi.
  west
715/654-6377
Open Fri.-Mon. or by appointment

Amery, Wisconsin

The Country School
Dorothy Bergstrand
Antiques, collectibles, candies,
  cheese and sausage
On. U.S. Hwy. 8, Rt. 3 54001
715/268-2987

Appleton, Wisconsin

The Hodge-Podge
Doris and Bob Geyer
Antiques, collectibles, appraisals
106 E. Franklin St. 54911
414/733-5901

Ashland, Wisconsin

The Antique Inn
Mr. and Mrs. Frank J. Myott
Antiques, candy, cheese
2016 E. Front St. 54806
715/682-5452

Beaver Dam, Wisconsin

Everybody's Attic
Ruth Hoeft
General line antiques and
  collectibles
1021 N. Spring St. 53916
414/887-2981

Beloit, Wisconsin

Granny's Attic
Elizabeth C. Mason
Antiques and gifts in country store
  atmosphere
1111 Madison Rd. (triangle of
  Liberty and Madison Rd. on Hwy.
  213N) 53511
608/362-6328
Tues.-Fri. 12 to 8
Sat.-Sun. 1 to 5
Mon. By chance

Reed-Warner American Antiques
Josephine Reed Warner
1217 Bushnell St. (west off I-90)
  53511
608/362-4558
Appointment suggested
W.A.D.A.

Burlington, Wisconsin

Johnston Antiques
Old Bellcroft House
P.O. Box 93, Spring Prairie Rd.
  53105
2 mi. west of Burlington, 1 mi. north
  of Hwy. 11, just west of DD
414/763-7258
W.A.D.A.

Stoffels' Antiques & Uniques
Anne J. Stoffels
Rt. 5, Box 58 53105
Between Burlington & Hwy. 50
  on 83
414/537-2335
W.A.D.A.

Camp Douglas, Wisconsin

Mill Bluff Antiques
Gladys E. Bergs
Furniture, glassware, copper
Rt. 2 54618
1 mi. west of Mill Bluff State Park
  on Hwys. 12 and 16 between Oakdale and Camp Douglas, then ½
  mi. south on side road, second
  place
608/427-6728

Cassville, Wisconsin

The Browse Shoppe
Paul Richter
Main St.
608/725-5644

Cedarburg, Wisconsin

Dorothy Gallun Antiques
General line
P.O. Box 43
1034 E. Bridge St. 53012
414/377-9250
W.A.D.A.

Centerville, Wisconsin

West Prairie Square
Janet Ecker
Primitives and glassware
3 mi. west of Centerville
608/539-2582
Open 6 days 10:30 to 5:30
Mon. by appointment

Chippewa Falls, Wisconsin

White Cottage Antiques
Marianna Hanson
General line
Rt. 5, Box 474 54729
715/382-4242
Summer: daily 1 to 5 except Tues.-
  Wed. Winter: by chance or
  appointment
W.A.D.A.

Cleveland, Wisconsin

Raven Nest Antiques
Gerald Shafranski
6 rooms in a Victorian farmhouse
Rt. 1 53015
414/693-2801
W.A.D.A.

Clintonville, Wisconsin

Anita's Antiques
Oak Grove Rd. near County Rd. D
715/823-3094
By appointment or chance

Cooksville, Wisconsin

Only Yesterday Shop
19th century antiques
Rt. 2 Stoughton 53589
½ mi. east of Cooksville on Hwy. 59
608/873-7768, 873-6089
W.A.D.A.

The Red Door Shop
Eunice and George Mattakat
Evansville Route 1 53536
On Hwy. 138 at Cooksville
608/882-5911
Closed Mon.-Tues.
W.A.D.A.

Delafield, Wisconsin

The Encore Shop
Evelyn Schoen
Antiques, furniture, glassware
630 Milwaukee St. 53018
414/646-8738

Dickeyville, Wisconsin

Jane's Antiques
Furniture, china, glassware
Box 187 53808
1½ mi. south on Rts. 61 & 151

Dodgeville, Wisconsin

The Woodshed Antiques
Bill Treweek
Country antiques
5 mi. north of Dodgeville on
  Hwy. 23
608/935-3896
W.A.D.A.

Dorchester, Wisconsin

Sara's Antiques
Franklin and Sara Ludwig
54425
3 mi. north of Dorchester Corners
  on Hwy. 13, then 3 mi. west
715/678-2764

Dresser, Wisconsin

Pete's Emporium
Antiques, appraisals
54009
715/755-2159

Edgerton, Wisconsin

Mildred's Antique Shop
Mildred Harrison
20 N. Henry St. 53534
608/884-3031, 884-8718
W.A.D.A.

Elkhart Lake, Wisconsin

Siebken Resort Antique Shop
Mrs. O.S. Moeller
On the lake, 2 blocks from Hwy. 67
  53020
414/876-2600
W.A.D.A.

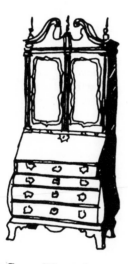

Elm Grove, Wisconsin

The Antique Lantern
Ginny and Russ Gonnering
Lighting and accessories
910 Elm Grove Rd. 53122
414/784-1760, 476-1761
W.A.D.A.

Ephraim, Wisconsin

Anderson House Workbench
Richard and Sally Hoyerman
Antique furniture, copper, brass
54211
On Hwy. 42, in historic Anderson
  House, built by Aslog Anderson,
  one of founders of Ephraim
May to Nov. 9 to 5, 7 to 9 daily,
  except Sun. 10 to 4

Louis Bungener
Residence: 914 S. Quincy St. 54301
Green Bay
414/432-7352
Shop: Ephraim 414/854-4159
W.A.D.A.

Red Barn Antiques
M. Binder, B. McAghon, S. Wright
Primitives, china, silver, collectibles,
  handpainted tinware
Rt. 42 54211
414/854-2045
10 to 5, May thru Oct.
North Wisc. A.D.A., N.A.D.A.

Evansville, Wisconsin

Magnolia House Antiques
Charles Shannon
4 mi. south on U.S. 213, Rt. 2
608/882-5666

Fish Creek, Wisconsin

The Pit & The Pendulum
Refinished antiques, lamps, and
  children's items
At the Fish Creek entrance to
  Peninsula State Park
7 days 8 a.m. to 10 p.m.

Fond du Lac, Wisconsin

The Victorian House
Antique furniture and decorative
  accessories displayed in a Victorian
  home
197 Sheboygan St. 54935
Daily 1-4:30 except closed Sun.

Fountain City, Wisconsin

Red Lantern Antiques and Strippers
Norman Berube
Large selection of antique furniture
608/687-9751
10 to 5 Sun.-Wed.

Friendship, Wisconsin

Friendship Antiques
Foy and Eloise Kneisel
Large general line, estates purchased
Hwy. 13, Main St. 53934
608/339-3130
Daily 9 to 5:30 except Sun. 11 to 5:30
W.A.D.A.

Galesville, Wisconsin

The Little Red Shed
Jackie Siefkas
Antiques, primitives, crafts
RFD 1
10 to 6 except Mon. and Thurs. by
  appointment only

Genesee Depot, Wisconsin

The Weathervane
Rosemary Beutner
P.O. Box 125 53127
Wed.-Sat. 11 to 5

Germantown, Wisconsin

The Black Horse Antique Shop
Furniture, primitives and collectibles
Hwy. 145-N,116-W, 15830 Main
  St. 53022
414/251-8315, 251-0815
Tues.-Thurs., Sat. & Sun. 12 to 5
  Fri. til 9
  Closed Mon.
W.A.D.A.

Mardi's Antiques
W 156 N 11606 Pilgrim Rd. 53022
Just off Hwy. 145
414/251-1244
Daily 11 to 5 except closed Mon.
W.A.D.A.

Hartford, Wisconsin

Audrey Marty
Holly Hill area
On Hwy. 83, ½ block south of
  Hwy. 167
414/673-4680
Open daily 10 a.m.
W.A.D.A.

Hustisford, Wisconsin

The Country Peddler
Sally and Walter Schockmel
312 W. Juneau St. 53034
414/349-3423
W.A.D.A.

Janesville, Wisconsin

Century Farm Antiques
The Rischs
Rt. 5 Cemetery Rd. 53545
1½ mi. west of Afton Rd. (County
  D) between Janesville and Beloit
608/752-0092
Daily 10:30 to 5:30 except Sun. 1 to
  5:30
W.A.D.A.

Jaeger Antiques
Country furniture over 100 years old;
  glassware
459 S. Randall Ave. ½ mi. off I-90
  53545
608/754-8585
W.A.D.A.

The Treasure Shop
Retta Messerschmidt
2116 Wesley Ave. 53545
608/752-6039
W.A.D.A.

Kenosha, Wisconsin

Farm Bell Antiques
Ruth H. Hall
10416 Green Bay Rd. 53140
414/694-2603
W.A.D.A.

Blue Spruce Antiques
W. Eric Dixon
4333 85th St. 53140
414/694-1714
By chance or appointment
W.A.D.A.

Lake Geneva, Wisconsin

The House of Treasures
Alyce and Lou Nesslar
General line, specializing in the
  unusual
P.O. Box 89 53147
414/248-8333
By appointment only
W.A.D.A.

Lake Tomahawk, Wisconsin

Eagle Lake Antiques
Lou Gillingham
Box 115 54539
715/277-2198

Lomira, Wisconsin

Martin House Antiques
Specializing in refinished furniture
½ mi. south of Lomira on 175
414/269-4455
Open Mon.-Wed. Other times by
  chance
W.A.D.A.

Lone Rock, Wisconsin

Ron Ferguson Antiques
Furniture, china, lamps, toys
Rt. 1, 53556
14 mi. east of Richland Center on
  Hwy. 14
608/583-3046

Lynxville, Wisconsin

Curiosity Shop
Wes and Carolyn Sampson
Furniture, glassware, collectibles
608/874-4339

Madison, Wisconsin

Buffalo Shoppe
Jerry Glaeve, Bonnie Edelstein
American furniture 1850-1920;
  stripping and refinishing service;
  large selection Wis. books
2530 Monroe St. 53711
608/233-3900
Mon. thru Sat. 9:30-5:30

Kappel's Clock Shop
Karl Kappel
Antique clocks, repairs
2250 Sherman Ave. 53704
608/244-6165; 238-3350

Old Madison Antiques
Full line of antiques
1348 Williamson St. 53703
608/251-2040
9:30 to 5:30 Tues.-Sat.

What Would Mother Say?
Jim Babcock
Period furniture, primitives, oriental,
  arts and crafts
422 North St. 53704
608/241-0453
Tues. thru Sat. 10 to 6 or by
  appointment

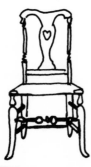

Madison, Wisconsin

The Last Straw
Joan B. Pruess
Refinished furniture (early 1800s,
  primitive, Victorian), glassware,
  jewelry, silver, decorator accessories
Large inventory at a second location
  (barn) by appointment
608/238-5991
4337 Mineral Point Rd. 53705
  (Westgate Shopping Mall at the
  Wallpaper Shoppe)
608/274-2077
Mon.-Fri. 9 to 9; Sat. 9 to 5;
Sun. 12 to 5

Mapleton, Wisconsin

Nancy Andrich Antiques
Rt. 1 Box 64-A Rubicon 53078
4 mi. north of Mapleton on Hwy. P
414/474-4593
By appointment
W.A.D.A.

Marinette, Wisconsin

Parasol Antiques
Carmen Kraft
2154 Riverside Ave. 54143
715/735-5464

Mazomanie, Wisconsin

Misty Valley Antiques
Theodore and Virginia Bast
Rt. 1, Mahocker Rd. Box 442 53560
Hwy. 14, 1 mi. west of Mazomanie,
  turn south ½ mi. on Mahocker Rd.
608/795-2849

Milwaukee, Wisconsin

Dorothy Taylor's White Shutters Shop
Frank and Dorothy Taylor
771 N. Jefferson St. 53202
414/271-8866, 332-3164
W.A.D.A.

East-Way Antique Shop
Carol Paulson
General line, steins
845 N. Marshall St. 53202
414/272-2640
W.A.D.A.

Laurette's Antiques
Mr. and Mrs. Phil J. Dreis
General line, dolls, jewelry, cut
 glass, souvenir spoons
414/771-7444
W.A.D.A.

Mid-America Antique Center
General line—furniture, lamps,
 glassware, china, jewelry
75 antique dealers under one roof,
 3 floors of antiques, 20,000 sq. ft.
341 N. Milwaukee 53202
414/276-0605
10 to 5 Mon. thru Sat.
1 to 5 Sun.

Virgie's Antiques
510 W. Riverview Dr. 53209
414/228-8314
W.A.D.A.

Mineral Point, Wisconsin

Mineral Point Antique Shop
Harry J. Kies
502 State St. 53565
608/987-3617

Mt. Horeb, Wisconsin

Keller Trading Co.
Wallace Keller
General line antiques, glass-topped
 wagon wheel tables, reproductions
209 E. Main St. 53572
608/437-5071; 437-8219

Monches, Wisconsin

Monches Country Store
Nancy Woll
Rt. 2, Box 118, Hartland 53029
N. of Hartland on E, W. of Meno-
 minee Falls on Q
414/628-1680, 966-2443
W.A.D.A.

Muskego, Wisconsin

Richard and Pat Olson
W 183 S8922 Racine Ave. 53150
414/679-2435
By appointment only
W.A.D.A.

New Holstein, Wisconsin

Spetta's Inc.
Jim and Randy Spetta
Auction service
Rt. 2, Box 151 53061
414/849-2932

North Fond du Lac, Wisconsin

The Sign of tne Rooster
Herman and Elizabeth Hahn
Collectibles
624 Michigan Ave. 54935
414/922-6407

North Lake, Wisconsin

Old North Church
Box 97 53064

Oakdale, Wisconsin

The Silver Teapot
Mary Gnewikow
Antiques and collectibles
North on PP at Oakdale village
  limits
608/372-6156

Oconomowoc, Wisconsin

Ye Old Antiques
Edward Weide
"Barns full" of furniture, primitives,
  glassware
38726 McMahon Rd. 53066
At Oconomowoc. north on Hwy. 67
  3½ mi. to McMahon Rd., turn west
  ½ mi.
414/474-4380

Oshkosh, Wisconsin

The Antique Corner
P.K. Williams
Furniture, china, glass, books,
  clocks, collectibles
802 Oregon St. (Bus. 41, US 45)
Mon.-Sat. 10 to 5
Closed Sun.

Palmyra, Wisconsin

Estate Services
American furniture, primitives,
  glassware
210 2nd St. (Between Milwaukee
  and Madison)
414/495-2649, 495-2604
Wholesale Mon.-Sat.
Auction 2nd and 4th Mon. each
  month 11 a.m.

Platteville, Wisconsin

Schneller's Antiques
620 Ridge Ave. 53818
608/349-6501

Racine, Wisconsin

The Frightened Hare
Terry and Angela Brintoɪ
Country furniture, lamps,
  accessories
1557 S. Green Bay Rd.   Hwy. 31
414/633-7035
By appointment only

Random Lake, Wisconsin

The Salt Box House
W. Allen and Bernice Wendel
53075
Rt. 1 Hwy. 144 & 28, 6 mi. west of
  Random Lake, 9 mi. north of West
  Bend
414/692-2649
By chance or appointment
W.A.D.A.

Ripon, Wisconsin

Second Hand Store
Antiques and used furniture
Hwy. 23 West 54971
414/748-3723; 294-3205

Rhinelander, Wisconsin

Cloudscape
Antiques
715/282-5566

Shawano, Wisconsin

Meadowcrest Antiques
Marjorie W. Klein
General line
P.O. Box 288 54166
East on Hwys. 29-47-55 at Co.
  Trunk E
715/526-2210
W.A.D.A., N.A.D.A.

Shawano, Wisconsin

Salt Cellar Antiques
Jacky Popp and Phyllis Tinsman
1345 Zingler Ave. 54166
715/526-5645
By chance or appointment
W.A.D.A.

Sheboygan, Wisconsin

Two in the Attic
Antiques and collectibles
M. Pearce and C. Sanders
Rt. 3, Bus Hwy. 131 S. 53081
414/452-5424
Tues.-Sat. 10 to 8
Sun. 12 to 6
Closed Mon.

Sister Bay, Wisconsin

The Rail Fence
Ron and Ethel Bitters
Hwy. 57, 1 mi. south of Jct. Hwy 42
414/854-4654
W.A.D.A.

Stoughton, Wisconsin

Neal's Antiques
Neal H. Larsen
Furniture, china, glass, lamps
417 Lowell St. 53589
608/873-3653

Sturgeon Bay, Wisconsin

1776 Shop
Richard and Sally Hoyerman
Restored antique furniture, copper,
  brass, hand-leaded glass reproductions
3rd Ave. Mall 54235
414/743-6734
Mon. thru. Sat. 9:30 to 5; Fri. 9:30
  to 9

Superior, Wisconsin

Curiosity Shop Antiques
Vivian and Bob Plunkett
Complete line of antiques
2331 Tower 54880
715/394-4080
Mon.-Sat. 9 to 5

Tiffany, Wisconsin

The Merry-Go-Round Shop
Harold and Rachel Teubert
Antiques and collectibles
53592
4 mi. west of 140, 6 mi. east of 51
  Creek Rd.
608/752-3196

Tomah, Wisconsin

Esther's Antiques
Esther Schendel
Primitives, glassware, bottles,
  collectibles
120 W. Saratoga St. 54660
608/372-6690
By chance or appointment

Van Dyne, Wisconsin

Bergman's Brown Cabin Antiques
Antiques and collectibles
425 Van Dyne Rd. Hwy. 175 54979
414/688-2665
By chance or appointment

Watertown, Wisconsin

Frieda Anne Lehmann
Antiques, china, glassware,
  collector's items
1018 E. Main St. 53094
414/261-3182

Watertown, Wisconsin

River Road Antiques
Marge and Dick Rowe
R.R. 4
2½ mi. off Hwy. 26 south of
  Watertown on County Y
414/261-3194

Waukesha, Wisconsin

Antiques
Robert H. Kruger
Mainly wholesale. Furniture, glass,
  china, lamps, collectibles
401 Madison St. Hwy. 18 at 104
  53186
414/542-7722
Daily 9 to 5

Judie Pieper Antiques
General line, featuring large selection of country store tins, signs,
  and boxes
437 E. North St. (Hwy. 164) 2½ mi.
  south of I-94
Daily 10:30 to 5
Sun. 1 to 5

Waupun, Wisconsin

The Donald Wm. Hallocks
222 Carrington St. 53963
414/324-2209
Appointment suggested
W.A.D.A.

West Salem, Wisconsin

Old Salem House, Inc.
General line, glass, porcelain, silver,
  lamps
99 Jefferson St. 54669
  Near I-90 interchange
608/786-1675

Weyauwega, Wisconsin

Deer-Crossing Antiques
Mrs. R. E. Peterson
Rt. 1 54983
6 mi. east of Waupaca on Hwy. 54
414/867-3513
By chance or appointment

Whitewater, Wisconsin

The White Elephant Shop
Elaine and Dick Hackett
Antiques, used furniture
183 W. Main St. 53190
414/473-4140

Wisconsin Dells, Wisconsin

Edmonds-Clasen Antiques
Rt. 2, Box 59 53965
7 mi. north of Dells on Hwy. 13
Open daily
W.A.D.A.

Woodruff, Wisconsin

The Mill Antiques
Dennis and Nancy Howard
Large selection of antiques,
  collectibles
Box 45 54568
715/356-5468
Open year round

 Canada

Canadian antiques that are at least 100 years old are not subject to duty or sales tax. To transport them across the U.S.-Canadian border without paying these taxes (20 and 12 percent, respectively), you will need a written statement from the dealer certifying the age of the articles you have purchased. The Canadian Antique Dealers Association, formed in 1967, has some 40 members in Ontario alone. The sign of the Association in a dealer's shop is assurance that your invoice will include a fair description of the article and that the dealer is expected to live up to high ethical standards. Members are indicated in this listing by the abbreviation "C.A.D.A." Of course, a dealer does not have to belong to the Association to operate by similar standards.

Pioneer life in mid-19th century Ontario has been recreated in Upper Canada Village, located in Morrisburg, south of Ottawa on the St. Lawrence River. This large restoration project is one of several in the province that preserve the history of the region.

Frances Kidd, a wholesaler who sells to dealers only, reports that in and around Barrie, Ontario (north of Toronto), there are many good antique shops, as well as auctions and flea markets. There are still lots of antiques in the area, she says—and besides, it's "beautiful country."

Arnprior, Ontario

Pine Farm Antiques
R.R. 2
40 mi. west of Ottawa, halfway between Arnprior & Renfrew, on Hwy. 17 (half a mile at Calabogie turnoff)
613/623-5716

Barry's Bay, Ontario

Madawaska Valley Antiques
Antiques, novelties, gifts
Combermere (Hwy. 62)
613/756-5044

Bath, Ontario

Millinocket House
Millhaven, Box 185
613/352-5830
C.A.D.A.

Belleville, Ontario

Leeman's Antiques
Eileen Leeman
General line antiques, furniture, glass, china, jewelry, silver, Canadiana
"In the heart of Prince Edward County one of the early settled areas of Ontario" (This area is known for its early handmade furniture, and there is still a quantity of local pine, butternut, cherry and dark wood furniture.)
R.R.1, Rednersville Rd. (take Hwy. 14 south off Hwy. 2; turn right off Bay Bridge; 1 mi. up the bay shore)
613/962-8184
By chance or appointment

Brantford, Ontario

Ox-Bow Antiques
Owned by Galloway Antiques Ltd.
English imports (furniture, clocks,
  glass, etc.), some Canadiana
R.R. 3
Ox-Bow Rd., first turn over Cock-
  shutt Bridge south out of Brantford
Located on a farm
519/752-2043
Daily 11 to 5 except closed Sun.

Brighton, Ontario

The Breakaway Antiques
Jill Guertin
Early Ontario furniture, mostly in
  the rough; primitive tools, books
  and paintings
R.R. 7 (2½ mi. north of Hwy. 401
  on Hwy. 30)
613/475-2671
By chance or appointment

Burgessville, Ontario

Pig 'n' Plow Antiques
Marjorie Larmon
R.R. 1
519/424-9997
C.A.D.A.

Carleton Place, Ontario

Country Corners
Furniture, antiques, restoring,
  refinishing
Black's Corners, R.R. 2
613/257-1030

Collingwood, Ontario

Collingwood House Antiques
Bill and Carol Bowden
Period and primitive furniture,
  clocks, light fixtures, lamps, glass,
  china, tools
280 First St. (on Hwy. 26 in town)
705/445-4088
Winter: Thurs.-Sun. 10 to 5
Summer: Tues.-Sun. 10 to 5
Closed Mon. unless a holiday
Area has historic sites, skiing,
  fishing, boating

Dundas, Ontario

The Green Door
A.E. Lewis
Antiques, fine furniture, crafts
6 Cross St.
416/628-6712
10 to 5:30 except closed Sun. and
  Mon.

Elginburg, Ontario

Blake McKendry Limited
Antique Canadian furniture,
  Canadian art, folk art
Latimer Rd. (near Kingston)
613/353-2120
By chance or appointment

Galt, Ontario

R. Leslie Donaldson
13 Salisbury Ave.
519/621-8189
C.A.D.A.

Gananoque, Ontario

Beaver Hall Antiques
21 King St. E.
613/382-2228
C.A.D.A.

Hamilton, Ontario

Ten Mile House
Canadian pine furniture
555 York
416/525-7796

Hillsburgh, Ontario

Old Inn Antiques
Canadiana and pine furniture
519/855-4506

Kettleby, Ontario

Ancient Canada Antiques
Mr. and Mrs. R.S. Geue
416/727-4111
C.A.D.A.

Kingston, Ontario

The Cottage Antiques
Mr. and Mrs. T.A. Lewis and Mr.
   P.A. Lewis
General antiques, specializing in
   refinished pine furniture
326 University Ave.
613/542-6189
Daily 10 to 4:30

Kirkton, Ontario

The Collectors' Shop
George and Harold Burgin
Antiques, used furniture, farm tools,
   gas engines, specializing in bottles
   and fruit jars
Hwy. 23, halfway between London
   and Stratford, Ont.
(Shop was formerly a large
   hardware store)
519/229-8965
July, Aug. 7 days a week 1:30 to 6
Other 10 months Sat. 10 to 6;
Sun. 1:30 to 6

Lambeth, Ontario

Weldwood Antiques
Antiques and collectibles (retail and
   wholesale)
Wharncliffe Rd. S. between South-
   dale and Hwy. 135
519/652-5519; 652-2810

Lindsay, Ontario

Burridge Century House
Pleasant Point
R.R. 6
705 Dunsford 33R 15

London, Ontario

The Antiquarian
Anne Singer
Wicker furniture, primitives, stained
   glass windows, antiques and curio-
   sities, Victorian and art nouveau
   jewelry
361 Dundas St.
519/438-2333
10:30 to 3, closed Mon., or by chance
   or appointment (679-1451)

Beds 'n' Things
Brass beds, antiques, furnishings,
   restoration service
342 Dundas St.
519/438-3381

Greenland Farm Antiques
Helen Green
Large barn with primitives, old
  rough furniture, as well as fine fur-
  niture and glassware
North St., R.R. 1
519/471-0967
"Always open"
The last battle of the War of 1812
  fought on this site

Oblio's Canadian Country Furniture
567 Richmond
519/432-2141

Mallorytown, Ontario

Rusty Kettle
John Player
Country furniture, iron, tin
Box 259, R.R. 2
613/659-2753
By chance or appointment

Maple, Ontario

Black Walnut Shop
Marjory and Ralph Brown
Antique furniture, china, glassware,
  crafts, gifts
9201 Keele St., R.R. 1
416/669-9201
Daily 1 to 5 or by appointment

Markham, Ontario

Canadian Homestead Antiques
Mogens and Margaret Philip
Specializing in early Canadian
  furniture
R.R. 2
416/294-1314
C.A.D.A.

G.B. Garlatti Antiques
R.R. 2
416/294-4066
C.A.D.A.

R.G. Perkins & Son Antiques, Ltd.
12 Main St.
416/294-4766
C.A.D.A.

Mississauga, Ontario

A.V. Baron Antiques, Ltd.
Specializing in authentic 17th and
  18th century furniture from
  England, France and Spain
264 Dundas St. E., Cooksville
416/277-1591
Daily 10 to 5 except closed Sun.
  and Mon.
C.A.D.A.

Niagara Falls, Ontario

Oldë Country Antiques
Antiques and old furniture
4604 Erie
416/356-5523; 356-0421

Niagara-on-the-Lake, Ontario

Howe's Antiques
Margherita Howe
Antiques, prints, primitives
61 Queen St. (This is an historic
  town, the first capital of Upper
  Canada, well-preserved since
  early 1800s.)
416/468-3328
12:30 to 6:30 p.m. year round

Orleans, Ontario

Heritage Antiques
Victorian and Georgian furniture
  and collectibles
2006 Notre Dame
613/824-2244

Ottawa, Ontario

Antique Village
Allan Lobel
Imported furniture, Canadiana,
  collectibles, nostalgia, Navajo
  jewelry
844 Rank St.
613/236-6064
Mon.-Sat. 9:30 to 6 except Fri.
  to 9

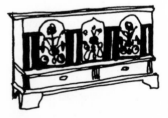

The Antique Shoppe
Period furniture, Canadiana furniture, china, glass, silver
767 Bank St.
613/232-0840
C.A.D.A.

Antique Village
Period furniture, Canadiana, art
  glass
844 Bank (at Fifth)
613/236-6064

Gora's House of Antiques Ltd.
French, English, Italian furniture;
  jewelry, silver, crystal, copper,
  pewter (wholesale and retail)
484 King Edward
613/235-4572

Mag and Peter's Store
"Ottawa's pre-1945 store—antiques,
  old furniture and junk"
395 Gladstone
613/233-9723

*The Old Vic Pine Antiques and
  Gallery*
Mrs. Shirley B. McIntosh
Pine furniture (armoires, dough
  boxes, clocks, etc.), Canadian
  paintings, fine period furniture,
  glass, silver, jewelry
327 Somerset West
613/232-8637

Yesterday-Century Old Furniture
Antiques and curios
281A Richmond Rd.
613/722-6222

Paris, Ontario

Canadiana Trading Post
Pat Gerbrandt
Refinished pine furniture and
 primitives from Ontario, Quebec,
 and the Maritime provinces
16 Broadway St.
519/442-6297
Open daily including weekends

Plattsville, Ontario

Henry Dobson Antiques
519/684-7434
C.A.D.A.

Port Credit, Ontario

Bonne Affaires Antiques
European and Canadiana furniture,
 clocks, guns, refinishing and
 restoration
316 Lakeshore Rd. E.
416/278-0335

Portland, Ontario

Willmark Antiques
Pine furniture, primitives, lamps,
 collectibles
Main and Colborne
613/272-2517

Scarborough, Ontario

*Collectors' Corner Historical
 Society & Antique Market*
1683 Kingston
416/691-6575

Shelburne, Ontario

Honey House Antiques Ltd.
Early Canadian furniture
511 Main E.
416/925-2324

Simcoe, Ontario

The Loft
Fern Brook
449 Norfolk St. S., Box 100
519/426-6670
C.A.D.A.

Smiths Falls, Ontario

Montague House Antiques
"For the collector and the beginner"
R.R. 4
613/283-1168

St. Catharines, Ontario

Adam Haynes Antiques
Pre-Confederation Canadiana in an
 early Canadian stagecoach inn
2 mi. south of Hwy. 8, on Fifth St.,
 Pelham Rd.
416/684-0019
C.A.D.A.

The Town House Antiques
216 King St.
416/684-1053
C.A.D.A.

St. George, Ontario

Gagnon Gaetan Antiques
Canadian antiques, pine and oak
  furniture
R.R. 1, Troy (Hwy. 5)
519/448-1158
Open 7 days 9 to 6

St. Thomas, Ontario

The Stag Antiques
"Authentic early Canadiana"
Talbotville
519/633-2320

Streetsville, Ontario

H. Manning Antiques
221 Queen St. S.
416/826-1754
C.A.D.A.

Toronto, Ontario

Avendale Antiques
Canadiana and country furnishing,
  restoration
104 Avenue Rd.
416/921-6140

The Bailiwick
Canadiana antiques and crafts, furniture refinishing, framing, brass
  and metal reconditioning
1627 Bayview Ave. (south of
  Eglinton)
416/489-1767

Henry Birks & Sons Antique Dept.
134 Yonge St.
416/366-7511
C.A.D.A.

Chance Jeanneret Limited
177 Avenue Rd.
416/922-1609
C.A.D.A.

The Chelsea Shop
386 Huron St.
416/923-7722
C.A.D.A.

Edward E. Denby
1206 Yonge St.
416/921-2493
C.A.D.A.

Robert Dirstein & Partners, Ltd.
77 Yorkville Ave.
416/961-6211-12-13-14
C.A.D.A.

The Gold Shoppe
85 Bloor St. W.
416/923-5564-65
C.A.D.A.

Diane Lander Antiques
183 Avenue Rd.
416/922-8361
C.A.D.A.

Lorenz Antiques, Ltd.
701 Mt. Pleasant Rd.
416/487-2066
C.A.D.A.

Harry MacDonald Ltd.
158 Davenport Rd.
416/922-3778
C.A.D.A.

Mish-Mash Market Ltd
Furniture, brass beds, clocks; "over
 1,000 interesting and unusual old
 items"
1023 Finch W. (at Dufferin in Plaza)
416/630-8486
Open 7 days

Pagnello's Antiques
All types of antiques, repairs, silver
 plating, brass polishing
1635 Bayview Ave. (at Eglinton)
416/488-8080

The Paisley Shop Ltd.
889 Yonge St.
416/923-5830
C.A.D.A.

R.G. Perkins & Son Antiques Ltd
1198 Yonge St.
416/925-0973
C.A.D.A.

The Robert Simpson Co. Ltd.
 (department store)
Treasure House
176 Yonge St.
416/861-6088
C.A.D.A.

Carol Solway Antiques
88 Yorkville Ave.
416/922-0702
C.A.D.A.

The Source Antiques
Specializing in pub paraphernalia
 stained glass, mirrors and brass,
 chairs and furnishings
746 Mt. Pleasant
416/487-7607

*Budd Sugarman Interior Design &
 Antiques Ltd.*
19 Hazelton Ave.
416/925-4471
C.A.D.A.

Michel Taschereau Antiques
116 Avenue Rd.
416/923-3020
C.A.D.A.

Toronto Antiques & Art
Canadiana, Victorian, Ontario furniture
1647 Kingston (just east of Warden)
416/698-1368

Ross Antiques
Specializing in Victorian furniture
2279 Bloor W. (east of Windermere)
416/767-0055

Upper Canada Antiques
Early Canadian furniture
590 Markham
416/536-8667

Upper Canada House
Canadian furniture, prints and
  accessories
467 Eglinton W.
416/489-9110
C.A.D.A.

Ronald Windebank Antiques
180 Avenue Rd.
416/962-2862
C.A.D.A.

Vineland, Ontario

Barclay Holmes Antiques
P.O. Box 534, Chestnut Hall
Victoria Ave. S.
416/562-5316
C.A.D.A.

Waterdown, Ontario

The Hilltop Furniture & Antiques
Mrs. Rita J. Vanderzee
Furniture, primitives, new brass beds
Hwy. 586, Clappison Corners
  (near Hamilton)
416/689-6555
7 days, 11 to 6

Windsor, Ontario

Green Gables Antiques
Canadian primitives, etc.
1277 George
519/945-4529

Lettner's (Pearce Lettner Ltd.)
345 Ouellette Ave.
519/253-8465
C.A.D.A.

Margaret Moran Studio
English and Canadian antiques,
  collectibles, gifts
5837 Wyandotte E.
519/945-0836

Those Oldies But Goodies
Antiques and good used wood
  furniture
505 Wyandotte E.
519/253-6183

Bibliography — Books

Andrews, Edward Deming and Faith. **Religion in Wood.** Bloomington: Indiana University Press, 1966.

Bjerkoe, Ethel Hall. **The Cabinetmakers of America.** Garden City, N.Y.: Doubleday & Company, Inc., 1957.

Comstock, Helen. **American Furniture.** New York: Viking Press, 1962.

Davidson, Marshall B. **The American Heritage History of Antiques from the Civil War to World War I.** American Heritage Publishing Co., Inc., 1969.

Drepperd, Carl William. **Victorian, the Cinderella of Antiques.** Garden City, N.Y.: Doubleday, 1950.

Durant, Mary. **The American Heritage Guide to Antiques.** New York: American Heritage Press, 1970.

Eastlake, Charles Locke. **Hints on Household Taste.** New York, 1872.

Freeman, John Crosby. **The Forgotten Rebel: Gustav Stickley and His Craftsman Mission Furniture.** Watkins Glen, N.Y.: Century House, 1966.

Grotz, George. **The New Antiques: Knowing and Buying Victorian Furniture.** Garden City, N.Y.: Doubleday, 1970.

Ingolfsrud, Elizabeth. **All About Ontario Beds.** Toronto: The House of Grant (Canada) Ltd., 1975.

———**All About Ontario Chairs,** Toronto: The House of Grant (Canada) Ltd., 1974.

———**All About Ontario Chests.** Toronto: The House of Grant (Canada) Ltd., 1973.

Kovel, Ralph and Terry. **American Country Furniture.** New York: Crown Publishers, 1965.

Lea, Zilla Rider. **The Ornamental Chair: Its Development in America [1700-1890].** Rutland, Vt.: Charles E. Tuttle Co., 1960.

McClinton, Katherine Morrison. **Collecting American Victorian Antiques.** New York: Charles Scribner's Sons, 1966.

Maass, John. **The Gingerbread Age.** New York: Rinehart & Company, 1957.

Madden, Betty I. **Art, Crafts and Architecture in Early Illinois.** Chicago: University of Illinois Press, 1974.

Minhinnick, Jeanne. **At Home in Upper Canada.** Toronto: Clarke, Irwin & Company Limited, 1970.

Ormsbee, Thomas H. **Care and Repair of Antiques.** New York: Medill McBride Company, 1949.

———**Early American Furniture Makers.** New York: Thomas Y. Crowell Co., 1930.

———**Field Guide to American Victorian Furniture.** New York: Bonanza Books, 1952.

Otto, Celia Jackson. **American Furniture of the Nineteenth Century.** New York: Viking Press, 1965.

Palardy, Jean. **The Early Furniture of French Canada.** Toronto: Macmillan of Canada, 1963.

Ransom, Frank E. **The City Built on Wood.** Ann Arbor, Michigan: Edwards Brothers, Inc., 1955.

Shull, Thelma. **Victorian Antiques.** Rutland, Vt.: C.E. Tuttle, 1963.

Walters, Betty Lawson. **Furniture Makers of Indiana 1793 to 1850.** Indianapolis: Indiana Historical Society, 1972.

Way, Nelson E. and Constance Stapleton. **Antiques Don't Lie.** Garden City, N.Y.: Doubleday & Company, Inc., 1975.

Yates, Raymond F. and Marguerite W. **A Guide to Victorian Antiques.** New York: Harper & Brothers, 1949.

Journal articles and pamphlets

Furniture by New York Cabinetmakers 1650 to 1860. Museum of the City of New York, 1956.

The Furniture Trade Journal. Chicago: April, 1879.

The Western Furniture Trade. Chicago: August, 1876.

Van Ravenswaay, Charles. **"The Anglo-American Cabinetmakers of Missouri 1800-1850."** Missouri Historical Society Bulletin, April, 1958.

Widdicomb, William. **"The Early History of the Furniture Industry in Grand Rapids."** Historical Society of Grant Rapids, April 21, 1909.

Index

notes